12 KEYS TO
WRITING
BOOKS
T H A T
SELL

K A T H L E E N   K R U L L

ABOUT THE AUTHOR

Kathleen Krull began working in publishing the day after graduating *magna cum laude* from Lawrence University in Appleton, Wisconsin, and has survived fifteen years' editorial experience in commercial trade books, mass market books, textbooks, small press books, and books for the school and library market. From her most recent full-time job as Senior Editor at Harcourt Brace Jovanovich, she retired at age thirty-two to become a writer, freelance editor and consultant, gardener, piano player, and pleasure seeker in San Diego, California.

Her eclectic publishing credits range from the sacred to the profane: compiler and musical arranger for *Songs of Praise* (Harcourt Brace Jovanovich), an annotated collection of hymns based on her childhood as a church organist in Wilmette, Illinois; a 24-book concept series for young children (Raintree Publishers); *Sometimes My Mom Drinks Too Much* (Raintree), under the pseudonym Kevin Kenny; *What Will I Be?* (Western Publishing), an autobiographical Little Golden Book; books in the *Trixie Belden* mystery series for girls (Western), under the pseudonym Kathryn Kenny; articles and reviews for *The New York Times Book Review* and *Publishers Weekly*; and a piece called "Lady of the Evening," about the strangeness of mastering a computer while the rest of San Diego is asleep.

12 KEYS TO
WRITING
BOOKS
THAT
SELL

KATHLEEN KRULL

Writer's
Digest
Books

Cincinnati, Ohio

12 Keys to Writing Books that Sell. Copyright © 1989 by Kathleen Krull. Printed and bound in the United States of America. All rights reserved. No part of this book may be reproduced in any form or by any electronic or mechanical means including information storage and retrieval systems without permission in writing from the publisher, except by a reviewer, who may quote brief passages in a review. Published by Writer's Digest Books, an imprint of F&W Publications, Inc., 1507 Dana Ave., Cincinnati, Ohio 45207. First edition.

93 92 91 90 89   5 4 3 2 1

Library of Congress Cataloging-in-Publication Data

Krull, Kathleen.
    12 keys to writing books that sell/Kathleen Krull.
        p.   cm.
    Bibliography: p.
    Includes index.
    ISBN 0-89879-351-3
    1. Authorship. I. Title. II Title: Twelve keys to writing books that sell.
PN151.K77 1989   88-27134
808'.02 – dc19   CIP

*To Martha Hayes, Betty Ren Wright,
Jane Palecek and Russ Bennett, and
Joan Chase Bowden and Maria Modugno —
who got me jobs and enabled me
to think like an editor*

CONTENTS

READ THIS FIRST

*Authors should be required to walk a
mile in the shoes of those who work in
the publishing business.*
   — Leonard Felder (an author)

Some encouraging facts: During one five-month period in 1987, forty-five publishers published a total of 128 first novels, with small presses accounting for an even greater number — exact tally unknown. That same year, "books and maps" was the category of personal consumption expenditures showing the largest growth. A steady 20 percent of Americans continue to buy books: a sublime statistic in a time of VCRs, MTV, cable, dozens of new movies each month, more magazines than ever.

  More good news: Editors are on your side. "It is probably easier for a writer to get . . . published today than it has ever been," according to editor Jonathan Galassi. Says editor Patricia Gauch: "I love the slush pile."

  Still more good news: By answering that vexing question — "What do editors *want*?" — *this* book provides keys that will make the process of getting published quicker and more efficient.

KNOWLEDGE AND THE NEW WRITER

Every writer starts out naive and unpublished:

- Virginia Woolf, sending out her first article submissions, neglected to include her address and also didn't think to enclose the all-important SASE (self-addressed stamped envelope).

1

- Gail Godwin sent the *only* copy of her first novel to a publisher she hadn't researched—which turned out to have no
  office—and never saw the manuscript again.
- Jack London mailed out—and received rejections for—a
  dozen manuscripts before he learned that editors prefer
  typed, not handwritten, submissions.
- Raymond Carver got his first story typed, but he then submitted it to the magazine's circulation department, not the
  editorial address.
- Jack Kerouac typed *On the Road*, but on one continuous
  roll of pasted-together Teletype paper (the equivalent of
  neglecting to separate a continuous computer printout),
  causing such consternation to one publisher that he ended
  up with another.
- Bestselling author Mary Higgins Clark, prior to getting her
  current rate of $2+ million per book, has had her work
  rejected as "too slight."

Countless books considered classics today began their lives
with the same editorial acceptance and rejection process you
endure. To change rejection slips into contract offers, a writer
needs   courage,   persistence,   talent,   serendipity—and
knowledge.

Your goal, if you've picked up *this* book, is to sell your
manuscript or proposal to a mysterious being known as an editor. You *could* accomplish this by blind luck, ESP, voodoo, or
following today's horoscope.

Or, you could learn what an editor is going to think as
he or she reads your material. You could develop a working
knowledge of how publishing decisions are made. You could
troubleshoot your book now to short-cut the long and involved
submission process later. You could find out that it is *always* to
your advantage to know as much about editors and publishing
as you can.

This is a book that will show you how to think like a book
editor. Not so that you can *be* a book editor (unless you genuinely want to change careers), but so that you discover the keys
to what editors look for, which will enable you to do better what
you do best: write books—and then *sell* them. (In *this* book, the

term "book" includes fiction and nonfiction manuscripts, pro-posals, and queries that you are trying to sell to a book editor.) This book is for first-time authors and others who want to better understand the reasons for a book's acceptance or rejection.

WHY EDITORS ARE SO PICKY

"The editor is first, foremost, and last, only a reader," writes editor Peter Davison, to which must be added: a reader who asks questions.

Knowledge of the myriad questions editors ask before sign-ing your book will make you a publishing sophisticate, but more important, you will learn shortcuts and methods to get "yes" answers. The more of these questions that you know can be answered to an editor's satisfaction, the better your chance of making a sale.

Perhaps you will scoff. "Everyone knows editors make deci-sions depending on what they had for lunch," you might say. "I'm far too busy with my typewriter/word processor/quill pen to worry about an editor's mind. Editors should publish what I want to write. I shouldn't have to read their minds. *They* should be reading *mine*."

But book publishing, contrary to popular delusion, is not a philanthropic enterprise or a hobby for employees still sup-ported by their parents or a service industry for beginning writ-ers. Publishing is a *business*.

"Publishers exist to make money and make money to exist," writes small press editor Bill Henderson. You, the writer, are asking a publisher to invest money in your book—money that the publisher has only a 30 percent chance of earning back. (That's right: Seven out of ten published books either break even or lose money.)

Business decisions are not made according to writers' de-mands. They're not even made, I can tell you from fifteen years' experience, according to *editors'* moods and caprices (much less according to their menu choices at lunch).

"The publishing industry has no obligation to the writers

of America," says editor Gordon Lish. "So far as obligation goes, writers have it all." In other words, writers are more responsible for their successes and failures than they believe.

Writers who persist in expecting editors to publish whatever they write are handicapping themselves needlessly. *Editors publish books they know or hope the public will buy.* They have good reasons for knowing or hoping—reasons that are not difficult to learn. Their mode of thinking is logical and straightforward and not as intimidating as you might fear.

It's true: The odds against beginning writers are very high, but that's precisely because *many writers are not taking into account the questions editors ask.*

In the autobiographical *Martin Eden*, Jack London's turn-of-the-century hero is asked how great writers have *ever* succeeded with such "thinkless creatures" as editors. "They arrived by achieving the impossible," says Eden. "They did such blazing, glorious work as to burn to ashes those that opposed them. They arrived by course of miracle."

Working miracles is considerably easier in the late twentieth century, with a pulsating small press scene and a surging number of guides written for writers (whereas Eden triumphed via harrowing experience, and London himself, after his *600 rejections*, has become the most widely translated author in America).

HOW TO USE THIS BOOK

These twelve chapters will walk you through the maze of editorial questions, both obvious and obscure, that editors ask when deciding which books they want to publish. Each chapter begins with information a writer needs to know, and ends with explicit directions for getting to the "yes" answer, with occasional true stories in between.

Some questions you may have thought were important won't even be on this list. A few of these questions you may already be aware of. Many of them will surprise—and possibly even shock—you.

These twelve keys to getting published are not necessarily

of equal importance—the length and placement of each chapter are rough indications of the relative weight of each question in the editor's mind. Information regarding one question may also be applicable to others. Not all of these questions are asked about each and every book, but getting published requires at least an awareness that they exist.

Twelve is, as you might guess, an arbitrary number. Some editors have fewer questions, some have more. (For those who suspect that contemplation of twelve questions will prove the writerly equivalent of Chinese water torture: In its original incarnation as a lecture I used to give at universities, this list had *thirty-three questions*.)

Many of these questions are not even asked at the conscious level, but instead are answered all at once in the famous editorial hunch. (That's hunch, not lunch.) But hunches are not born of thin air—editors live with these twelve questions (or more or fewer) every day of their working lives.

An acquiring editor, a hypothetical Edward or Edwina (hereafter known as the unisex Ed), opens your package and immediately begins considering an ever-widening circle of questions. This book traces the same sequence as that thought process—which, unlikely as it may seem at first, does have a coherent progression:

• First and most numerous (Chapters 1 to 7) are the genuine editorial questions, starting with whether Ed even *likes* your book and feels it has some kind of literary worth. Is the manuscript physically neat, well organized, a pleasure to read? Do you write well? Do you have an opening sentence that grabs? Have you targeted a subject people will want to read about? Is it easy to envision your audience? Where did your ideas come from and are they fresh and original? Does the book meet Ed's needs? How much revision is necessary? Ultimately—per Question #1—is this what Ed would define as a *good book*? Unless the answer to that is "yes," the other eleven questions just don't get asked.

• Next Ed considers the marketplace (Chapters 8 and 9). Ed might love the book—will anyone else? Enough people to justify the expense of producing and marketing it? Have you demonstrated that it will meet a need in the marketplace? What makes you qualified to write this book? Will it make money for the company?

- Ed will then consider design and production factors (Chapter 10): Can the book be attractively designed and produced at a cost that allows the company to make a profit?

- Ed moves on to contemplate the field of subsidiary rights (Chapter 11), which can generate significant income for the company. Does your book have the potential to be excerpted to magazines or newspapers, or to sell to the movie or TV industry, foreign countries, book clubs?

- Finally, Ed will contemplate your backlist future, and the response of the literary and publishing community to your book (Chapter 12). Will it be favorably reviewed? Will it prove immortal — or at least stay in print for many income-producing years?

These final three chapters travel through potentially alien territory that will make the *most* sense to writers who have published one or more books. Still, the information is here, because editors take it into account at this time, and getting these landmarks in the publishing landscape in perspective now will come in very handy later in your career.

In any case, you now have some idea what editors do, and *why* it sometimes takes so long to hear from them. Choosing what to publish is not a simple process. Editors do not rely on their acumen alone, but will consult various people whose opinions matter. Also, depending on the company, editors usually submit their books to the approval of an editorial board — a committee of various people within the company. This puts editors in your position: selling your book to apathetic, overworked, or even hostile decision-makers.

But the editors — having worked their way through these twelve (or more or fewer) questions — are powerful advocates, and you, too, will be stronger for having thought these twelve keys through yourself. By reality-testing your own book's strengths and weaknesses, you've done some of Ed's thinking already, and you'll be that much further ahead in the submission process.

You can use the questions even more constructively: to understand possible previous rejections, and, having understood them, capitalize on them. You'll find out what the irritating phrase "not right for our list" actually means, and exactly how to get yourself *to* the right list.

Regardless of a company's size and policies, decisions about what to publish all start within the inquiring mind of an editor, and the next twelve chapters contain the keys to what you need to know to sell a book to that editor: the typical questions a typical editor asks about a typical book—and in roughly the same order every time.

And not just the questions, but the *answers*.

The most important thing, no matter how arcane and intimidating the editorial decision-making process may *seem*, is not to give up. As author Robert A. Heinlein stresses, the first rule for success in writing is that "you must *write*."

The aim of this book is not to frighten anyone to the point of discouragement, but to inspire writers to reach for greater heights and to write manuscripts that are more publishable. Editors are actively looking for you, and the market for publishable books, including yours, has never been healthier. Onward!

PART 1

EDITORIAL QUESTIONS

1. Is this a *good book*, or does it have that potential?
2. Does the book come alive?
3. Does the book have a clearly defined focus?
4. Does the book have a clearly defined audience?
5. Is the book original and fresh?
6. Does the book have integrity?
7. How much editorial work will the book require?

1.

IS THIS A *GOOD BOOK*, OR DOES IT HAVE THAT POTENTIAL?

There could be nothing so important as a book can be.
— *Maxwell Perkins*

The days of Maxwell Perkins (legendary editor for F. Scott and Zelda Fitzgerald, Ernest Hemingway, Thomas Wolfe, and many others) are not over yet.

Some sixty years post-Perkins, when fire alarms punctuated the gala 1988 book-awards ceremony of the National Book Critics Circle, New York book editors fled into the January evening frigidity without their coats—but not without their manuscripts.

Startled fire-fighters and police were helpless as editors actually defied them to retrieve manuscripts from the coatroom before exiting the building. Manuscript submissions, which editors almost always cart home from the office to read on their own time, still awaited their yes-or-no decisions, and these editors were taking no chances, fire or no fire.

There is *still* nothing so important as the book can be.

"In the beginning was the manuscript," writes editor William Targ, and in the beginning is the initial evaluation of that manuscript's worth. Generally speaking, no creative editing, marvelous jacket, exquisite paper and ink, appearances on talk shows, flurry of subrights activity, or quantity of hype will turn a bad book—or weak idea—into a good one.

The book comes first. Everything that happens to it after

acceptance is secondary. This is true whether it's a large commercial house or small independent press. (In fact, to *start* a small press, says Phil Wood of Ten Speed Press, "All you need is a good book.")

Different publishers define "good" in different ways, but deciding whether or not a proposed book is "good" is by far the most important question editors ask. Unless the editor says at least a qualified "yes" here, the other questions don't come up at all. Editors—this is the first of many times you will read this— are unbelievably overworked, with no time to spend on less-than-good manuscripts.

Making the good-book evaluation perhaps seems impossible for a mere mortal. Editors *are* mortal, not the "cunning arrangement of cogs" that Jack London despaired of, but they are also, by training or inclination, prepared to ask and answer this question . . . by registering signs both subtle and prominent.

THE GIANT EYEBALL

The editor, our androgynous Ed, opens your package and immediately begins inspecting it.

At this point, Ed is on your side; an editor really *wants* your book to be good, for a whole host of reasons, including the exhilaration of discovery and the resulting kudos to Ed. Maxwell Perkins himself didn't become "legendary" until he became in 1919 the *only* editor to deem F. Scott Fitzgerald's first novel, *This Side of Paradise*, a good book (Fitzgerald, incidentally, had racked up 122 rejections before this sale).

The minute it's apparent, however, that Question #1 can be answered with a "no," Ed fishes out your SASE, encloses some sort of letter, and mails your book back. Heartless as this may seem, it's in Ed's interest to move briskly. One editorial assistant estimates that he looked at some 15,000 proposals in three years, spending a minute or less on most. Editors do not use their time well or earn money for the company by contemplating books they're not going to publish.

First, Ed registers your physical presentation. If it's neat and professional, Ed is encouraged. If it's not, Ed is distracted.

Is your manuscript double spaced and cleanly typed on good white bond with sufficient margins? Or does it make use of a dim typewriter ribbon, onion-skin or erasable paper that fades to the touch, inscrutable or cheap dot-matrix type, a smudgy carbon copy or poor photocopy, or (horrors) handwriting? Is the material easy to follow and in order? Or are there messy erasures or arrows pointing every which way? Have you made the initial contact with Ed by phone (*don't*) instead of by writing? Have you enclosed an SASE or sufficient postage to return the material? If it's more than ten pages long, has it been mailed *flat*? Have you taken care to see that it holds together with the proper rubber band, clip, or sturdy box (no staples or binders)?

Perhaps Ed strikes you as absurdly picky, if not anal-retentive. Wouldn't an editor recognize the next Tolstoy, the next Judy Blume, even if the words were chicken-scratched in purple ink on pink paper, much less whether or not appropriate postage was attached?

Actually, probably not. Ed has been reading all day — galley proofs, manuscript revisions, copyedited manuscripts, jacket flaps, catalog copy, production schedules, memos, reports, letters, newspapers, magazines, trade journals, contracts and legalese of all sorts, royalty statements, profit and loss sheets, books from competing publishers.

An editor sometimes feels like one giant eyeball. "It's truly amazing," writes small press editor Richard Peabody, "that anyone lasts longer than three years in an editorial position without suffering complete and total sensory burnout."

What Ed needs, after a day of absorbing written information, is a giant dose of Murine, *not* a pile of cryptic manuscripts. Any less-than-professional element of your physical presentation tends to tax Ed's patience — not the mood you want in someone who's to look favorably on whatever substance that presentation conceals.

A clean presentation radiates confidence. One top agent criticizes writers who send "poor carbons or photocopies of first novels that aren't even finished. This shows no respect for and understanding of the pressures of the publishing business. And if the writer doesn't believe in the work, why should anyone?" Your goal is to get Ed to suspend disbelief, not have immediate doubts.

Also, physical amateurishness warns Ed that the writing and ideas in the book are probably equally careless. You are free to find Ed wrong here, but it's not a risk a writer who wants to get published will take. Other, pristine manuscripts await Ed's attention.

Assuming a spotless presentation, Ed next takes in the content of your cover letter. Is it an individually typed letter addressed to Ed by name and is Ed's name spelled correctly? Or is it (shudder) a form letter sent out to heaven knows how many editors? Do you indicate familiarity with the type of books Ed's company publishes? If you have had any prior contact with Ed (such as a "yes" to a query letter or a conversation at a writers' conference), this is the time to mention it.

Is your letter short, to the point, well written, and attention attracting? Have you indicated your credits and what qualifies you to write your book? Do you demonstrate awareness of your book's competition (if any) and why your book is necessary or superior? Is your tone cordial and fairly formal, or do you sound patronizing, intimidating, or presumptuous? An adversary relationship is *not* what Ed is looking for. Do you make weird, unprofessional requests, such as what size advance you want, or what artist you'd like for the jacket? (This is not the time or place to discuss either one.)

Have you included only the information necessary to help Ed evaluate your book, or have you burdened Ed with irrelevant sentiments? Do you try to "explain" or "defend" your book — as if your material doesn't speak for itself?

If your letter runs more than a page, something is probably wrong.

Usually, a bad cover letter will not in itself turn Ed off, but a good one can definitely work to your advantage, making Ed pant to see more. In a query letter — asking Ed if you can send along your material for consideration — signs of unprofessionalism will almost always cause Ed to say "no."

YOUR WRITING PERFORMANCE

Let's assume Ed is panting. Your writing style is the next aspect to absorb Ed's attention. "Style" includes such basics as grammar, spelling, and proofreading skills. Is your writing riddled with grammatical errors, misspellings, and typos? Even a few such monstrosities are an immediate affront to the finely tuned sensibilities of any editor, who is unlikely to proceed with material so obviously irresponsible.

It is challenging enough for literate people to get published; it is next to impossible for the semi-literate — who contribute an amazingly high percentage to Ed's daily mail.

Ed looks for evidence that you write well. "Genius," wrote F. Scott Fitzgerald, "is the ability to put into effect what is in your mind," and while Ed may be willing to settle for less than genius, your material must show at least some evidence of strong writing ability. "If the prose gives me a thrill," says editor Faith Sale, "the images make me tingle, I want to — sometimes even feel I *have* to — publish the writer."

Most editors are not necessarily writing teachers, but they *are* trained to recognize bad writing. They can tell whether you take your craft seriously.

Have you submitted a polished piece of work, or something that's obviously a rough draft? Have you weeded out cliches and sentences that make no sense? Are you communicating with a reader, or are you merely indulging yourself? Is your style literate, clear, contemporary, and energetic? Better yet, is it lively and witty? Is it full of action and life? Do you have a real flair for words? Do you have an *interesting* way of writing that makes Ed want to read more? Is your style appropriate to your material — a literary style for a novel, a simple and nonsentimental approach for a children's book, a straightforward mode for nonfiction, etc.? Is your style informative, entertaining, touching, or otherwise in tune with your intended audience? Is it smooth and consistent?

Next, Ed gets to your content. Do you have a *book*, or is this a padded magazine piece, a short story, a wisp of an idea? Will it still be relevant in a year's time, when the book comes out? Do you have a point of view, and is it legitimate and consistent? Are your facts well researched and verifiable? Do you have something original to say?

Is yours the type of book that has been or could be successfully published by Ed's company? Every editor "must be aware of the strengths of the house and publish to those strengths," writes editor Betty Prashker.

At last, Ed registers the total effect of your work, judging it as "a writing performance," in John Farrar's term. Do you have a *good book*, a good idea that informs your prose?

Or, can Ed readily conceive of revisions that will make real your book's potential? "It's a rare project," says publisher Peter Workman, "that automatically hits you as *successful* the moment it comes in." Thus part of Ed's job is to look at a manuscript not "as it is," in publisher M. Lincoln Schuster's words, but "as it can be made to be."

At this point, editors ascend to matters of tastes and needs unique to each editor. There are, however, standards that most editors have in common.

TRUE STORIES: HOW EDITORS THINK

As an editor who makes decisions (i.e., asks the twelve Questions) about books, I wait until I have a large chunk of quiet time with few interruptions. I read manuscripts at night, sometimes very late. I have to be in a certain mood: alert, sensitive, open to possibilities of all kinds, able to keep many factors in mind at the same time. Having worked up to this pitch, I make the most of it by reading all of that week's mail at once.

Tracing the byways—the *unedited* byways—of other people's thought processes is hard work. But I think about creative people sending me material, and I marvel at all their ideas—some I've perhaps had myself and never developed, and other ideas I never in a million years would have thought of on my own.

My method is to read carefully until the point I become bored or impatient, or lose trust in the writer, and then I skim, paying special attention to the last few pages. The first sentence of a manuscript is crucial, the first few paragraphs are crucial, and the first few pages are crucial. If any of these grab me, I will probably read all the way through the manuscript, even if I see problems with it.

But a book has to set me on fire before I vote "yes." I think of all the paperwork and persuasion that will keep me bustling between Point A (this manuscript) and Point B (finished book), not to mention Point C (taking care of the book once it's published).

Reading manuscripts is a visceral, emotionally charged experience, filled with potential for exhilaration, disappointment, anxiety, comedy. I feel a responsibility to the human beings whose work I'm reading. I know what acceptance or rejection can mean.

(For another view of manuscript-reading, see the autobiographical first chapter of *Sophie's Choice* by William Styron. It's enlightening, especially when Styron rejects *Kon-Tiki*, by Thor Heyerdahl, and has to watch it become a #1 bestseller for another company.)

Here is what I look for, in descending order:

- good writing, or literary merit
- something that makes me laugh, or even giggle or smile
- something that makes me cry, or that makes me *feel* anything
- something fresh and unusual, a sense of style, having something new to say
- as wide an appeal as possible, preferably universal
- evidence that the author knows the market, particularly my company's books
- in fiction, a good story with lots of action and good characterization
- in nonfiction, a solid, balanced treatment of topics of interest to me
- an element of controversy, or definite opinions
- relevance and a contemporary feel
- evidence that the author has thoroughly thought through the material

- clarity, sincerity, factual accuracy
- a feeling that the material could be popular ten or twenty years from now
- a professional attitude

These are the criteria I use in determining "Is this a *good* book?" Other editors will have additional criteria, but most of the above factors (to be explored in subsequent chapters) will appear on most editors' lists.

The same is true of the following factors that tend to turn an editor off, ranked roughly in order of their frequency:

- material that's clearly inappropriate to the publishing company (*the* most common reason for rejection — see "How to Get to the 'Yes' Answer" to Question #4 for how to research this) or that duplicates what we've already done (see Question #5)
- shallow or slight ideas (the second most common reason for rejection)
- books that remind editors of prior publishing failures
- books that get off to long, slow starts
- boring material, useless digressions
- cuteness, showing off
- signs that the author is not taking writing seriously
- ignorance of conventions appropriate to the particular genre
- any evidence of sexism or racism, stereotypes of any kind
- sloppy research methods
- humor that falls flat
- signs that the author expects the editor to "clean up" the material
- heavy-handed morals, preachiness
- poorly done fantasy that goes nowhere
- autobiography that's not made interesting to anyone but the author

You may wonder how any book could possibly contain all of the positive factors and avoid all of the negative ones. Good point: Most manuscripts *are* rejected at this stage. By far the majority of unsolicited manuscripts are simply not publishable.

"Publishers will tell you," says publisher Michael Joseph, "that every manuscript which reaches their office is faithfully read, but . . . at least fifteen out of twenty manuscripts can be summarily rejected, usually with safety. There may be a masterpiece among them, but it is a thousand to one against." Every publishing company will report its own percentages, but the essence of this statistic is true.

And yet unsolicited manuscripts do get into print; I myself accepted several (see Question #2). They get published because some writers are writing really good books, and good books will, with persistence, get published. *Every* author starts out "unsolicited" in the beginning.

Editors take their "mission" incredibly seriously, and if they can't publish a good book that comes their way, they'll route it to the right department or person, or sometimes even a rival company. Finding *good books* is what makes Ed's job worthwhile.

HOW TO GET TO THE "YES" ANSWER

In general, make the physical presentation of your cover letter and your proposal or manuscript as neat and professional as you can. Keep an exact duplicate of whatever you send to a publisher. Don't try to be cute or "different" with your initial presentation—you will only alienate the editor with purple ink on pink paper, or a cover letter that rhymes, or a fancy typeface that's hard to read, or a box of chocolates as a "subtle" bribe. After you know Ed, such maneuvers may be welcome (especially the chocolates), but in the beginning, Ed is looking for a good book, not an amusing correspondent.

Most of the basics of a well-tempered physical presentation (given earlier in this chapter) are matters of common sense, plus there are whole books written specifically on this topic (see Bibliography). Also note the explicit instructions in annual writers' manuals such as *Writer's Market* and *Novel & Short Story Writer's Market*. (Always use the current year's editions.)

A definite "don't" is to call Ed up on the phone and talk about the wonderful book you have written or planned. Talking is great on talk shows, but editors are *readers* and cannot have a meaningful discussion with new writers until they have read their writing.

It's also not helpful to query, "What kind of books are you looking for?" because Ed will invariably reply, "We're looking for good books," which leaves you where you started.

A miraculously simple beginning to selling your book is to address your letter to Ed by name. "Your work has infinitely more chance of being read if it is specifically directed to an editor by name," says a top editor.

And it has a much better chance of getting *accepted* if it's directed to an editor who shares your interests and tastes.

AN ORGY OF INFORMATION

Besides *Publishers Weekly* (more on this magazine in Question #4), *Writer's Market*, and *Novel & Short Story Writer's Market*, your best source for editors' names is *Literary Market Place*, which most libraries carry as a reference book.

Revised annually, *LMP* is a directory of all publishing companies in the United States and Canada and contains the names of all important editors and staff, addresses and phone numbers, number of books the company published last year, and how many it has in print. All of this is classified by geography, by field of activity, and by subject matter. (*LMP* also lists all writers' associations; a calendar of all book trade and writers' events; all book clubs and book review sources; agents and grants; literary awards, contests, and prizes—an orgy of information for the professional writer.)

Getting the editor's name right sounds trivial, but I for one can't think of a writer I published who got mine wrong. Mail addressed to my immediate predecessor in the job was understandable (although a simple phone call to the company switchboard would have brought the writer up-to-date), but not mail addressed to "Editor" or to editors who had died, retired, or left years before. "Dear Sir" letters were not read. Misspellings were an irritant: Someone obviously went to the trouble of looking it up, but couldn't be bothered to get it right, throwing doubt on the writer's research methods and motivation.

The goal is to try to send your book to an editor you "know." As in many other fields, "who you know" can open doors in publishing. One children's book superstar jokingly advocates "sleeping around" with editors, but there's no need to get carried away. Virginia Woolf's first novel went to her half-brother — who owned a publishing company. But a writer can "know" an editor from just about anywhere. It helps to have feelers out in all directions, looking for editors you can claim some connection to. Then mention that connection in your cover letter, explaining why you think your book is right for that editor.

Perhaps you've talked to or seen Ed speak at a writers' conference — a good bet, with 400 annual writing conferences in this country that provide excellent opportunities to get to "know" editors. You may have read an article published by Ed, or an article about a writer who raves about an editor by name. You see a reference in *PW* or a writers' magazine about Ed looking for certain types of books. Cultivate a publishing gossip grapevine — writers' groups, booksellers, librarians you know — to find out about editors. If an editor has ever written you a personal or encouraging letter about a manuscript, keep writing to that editor by name.

Your writing teacher may have good recommendations about editors and may even be willing to introduce you to his or her editor. Or check the "People" section in *PW* for editors promoted to new jobs and looking for new books to justify their promotions.

Via research, learn the names of editors who publish books you cherish or that resemble yours. Check the dedication or acknowledgments page to books you like to see if the editor is mentioned by name; sometimes *PW* will mention editors of current books by name; or make a brief call to a publishing company's editorial department to *ask* who edited a book you particularly like. Stephen King (who incidentally had four novels and sixty stories rejected on his way to success) used a variation of this method when he addressed his first novel to "the editor of the *Parallax View*," a book he admired.

Research on editors pays off. Just as writers are counseled

to write the kind of books they enjoy reading, so do "editors tend to contract the sort of books they themselves enjoy," write two top editors.

Editors are not created equal. Some are ethereal literary types; some aren't. "I always feel like the hooker at the convention," says editor Page Cuddy—"I *love* commerce. I *love* junk." Try to match your interests, your tastes, even your age, to Ed's. If your novel is young and hip, don't send it to the oldest editor in the company.

Authors have a legitimate interest, according to editor Nan Talese, in learning "the editor's reputation for staying with a house or moving along, as well as the publisher's commitment to other authors [that you respect]."

Finding the right editor is the key to getting published, just as finding the right book is the reason for Ed's existence. The right editor for you, says consultant Leonard Shatzkin, "is the quintessence of all publishing has to offer. Everything else is secondary." Editors want to feel that you have a solid reason for sending your work to their attention. (This is one reason why many editors dislike multiple submissions, whose destinations are frequently scattershot, rather than well thought out.) This isn't snobbery, it's human nature.

Think about how you select a typist, a babysitter, a divorce lawyer, or a doctor; you don't, as a rule, hire strangers or those without recommendations. Ed, whose career and reputation are on the line with each new acquisition, isn't overly attracted to strangers either. Indicating familiarity with Ed's reputation is one sign that you've done some homework, that you're not an amateur. (It's a comparatively minor advantage that it also happens to appeal to ego.)

A similar sign is, at the end of your letter, thanking Ed for reading your work. Once editors accept it, they'll be thanking *you*, but in the meantime it's not their job to read manuscripts they're not going to accept: They're doing you a favor, and simple courtesies are always appreciated.

BECOMING A GIANT EYEBALL

Try to read your work with the eye of your target editor. Check for errors of grammar, the sense of your material, and just plain typos. If you find problems, fix them *before* sending your work out. Don't hope that Ed won't notice, or even worse, that Ed will fix them for you.

Mailing a first draft is seldom to your advantage. Even if it strikes you as a perfect gem, sit on it until it *continues* to leave that impression. In the age of computers, revision has become as close to a pleasure as it's ever going to get, but whatever your writing mode, it works against you to send out something that hasn't been revised to the best of your ability.

There's no hurry. If your memory needs refreshing on good basic writing skills, reread E.B. White and William Strunk's *The Elements of Style* — still the best "short course" on how to write.

If you need brushing up on grammar, delve into Marjorie Skillin and Robert Gay's *Words into Type*, a concise and clear guide with one of the best indexes ever seen.

Proofread your material once, twice, and yet again. If proofreading is not your forte, try to get help.

Have an honest dialogue with yourself about whether or not you've got a good idea. A book has to have a really "strong reason for being," according to editor Thomas Congdon. "Too many times I have talked to authors and have found that even *they* weren't convinced about their own books."

Have you got a strong enough idea for a book, as opposed to material for a magazine piece? Solicit some opinions; have people that you trust read your work. Saul Bellow says that he has learned more from nonprofessionals' comments than he has from formal criticism of his work.

Are *you* truly excited about your book? Excited enough to persist through possibly numerous rejections, or to endure the "slings and arrows of outrageous fortune" that publishing a book sometimes represents?

Take the time to learn the conventions of your genre. If you're writing a sensitive literary novel, study current competitive books and try to figure out what got them published. Visit small press bookstores in larger cities, look over the novels published by various presses, study current directories to learn the styles and subject needs of publishers that interest you.

The same research methods apply to romances, mysteries,

true crime stories, fantasies, horror, westerns, nonfiction of all kinds, glitzy Hollywood novels, religious books, even pornography. In science fiction, for instance, "without broad reading experience in the field, through which one learns the specific reading protocols of the genre, you can't tell whether you are reading good SF or bad," says SF editor David Hartwell. In children's books, you must be familiar with current books, not the books you read as a child.

Reading widely is one prerequisite to writing well. "In order to write a good book," says Nobel Prize-winning author Joseph Brodsky, "a writer must read a great deal of trash — otherwise, he won't be able to develop the necessary criteria."

This is all part of researching your market, and will, among other benefits, enable you to answer the twelve questions editors ask.

WHY EDITORS NEED YOU

Market research will open one avenue after another to truly useful information — via books, writers' magazines and trade journals, writers' conferences, courses, local writers' groups, national professional organizations and their newsletters, guidelines that many publishers (especially in genres such as romance) will send you.

Writing — unlike computer programming, chemical dependency counseling, fine carpentry — always seems to be a field people think they can jump into with no preparation and be instantly successful. This fallacy particularly prevails in children's books, but it's a common thread to Ed's daily mail.

"Writers who excel," points out writer Barbara Goldsmith, "are no different from other champions, but common sense precludes the thought that without rigorous preparation one could leap into the role of ballet dancer, Olympic skier, lawyer, or surgeon."

All success takes an apprenticeship:

• Bestselling novelist Robin Cook, before writing a word, sat down and read 100 bestselling novels in a row.

• Top-selling author Mary Higgins Clark, a widow with five children to support, worked between 5:00 and 7:00 each morning for six years without an acceptance (accumulating forty rejections before selling her first story).

• Bestselling author Dean R. Koontz wrote four novels a year during his first seven years of writing; in twelve years he never took a weekend off.

• Karleen Koen, the "Houston housewife" who made headlines not long ago with the large advance for her first novel (*Through a Glass Darkly*), took five years and three drafts to do it.

• Not until her twentieth submission to *The New Yorker* did Bobbie Ann Mason gain an acceptance.

• Sally Beauman, the "first novelist" who received a $1 million advance for *Destiny*, had in fact published nine Harlequin romances prior to this big sale.

Studying the craft of writing, learning to write well before sending anything to a publisher—this is what will help get a "yes" answer here. Even good writers can have trouble getting published; the bad just clutter up the mails.

Publishable books will, with persistence, get published.

You need to connect with the right editor, and that need is reciprocal. "It is my observation," says writer Jon Riffel, "that no group can compare with the editors and publishers of the book world when it comes to a dedicated effort to reach out and lend a helping hand to developing talent."

Most editors would humbly agree. "In the business of art there is always dedication and caring," says editor Rust Hills. Says editor Joyce Engelson: "Publishing wouldn't collapse without editors; it *would* collapse without the person sitting at the typewriter, writing. It's all the author."

And all the author's *book*.

2.
DOES THE BOOK COME ALIVE?

*If I read a book that impresses me, I
have to take myself firmly in hand before I mix with other people; otherwise
they would think my mind rather queer.*
                                —Anne Frank

Good books have the power to make readers do strange and
wonderful things. An ultimate example: In the movie *Romancing
the Stone*, vicious South American drug runners threaten the
heroine. Her back to the wall, she inadvertently reveals her
identity: the popular novelist whose stirring stories have them
hooked in local read-aloud sessions. They stand back—and
spare her life.

Another example of the power of the written word to grab:
The novelist in Stephen King's *Misery* (a novel of delicious obser-
vations about editors) is trying to write while being held captive
by a psychopathic nurse. Unless he comes up with a novel that
has "*the gotta,*" his captor will continue "exercising editorial authority over his body"—every bit as horrible as it sounds.

The gotta, says King, makes "the needle of some internal
Geiger counter swing all the way over to the end of the dial." It
makes a person stay up to see how a chapter comes out, even
when a spouse is waiting upstairs in bed. It makes someone read
to the end of a book—until it's too late to cook dinner. It makes
a child read under the covers at night with a flashlight.

And it's a little-known fact that more editors read unsolicited manuscripts than will admit it in print. They're looking for *the gotta*:

- One editor started reading Jean Stafford's first-novel manuscript on the train home, looked up to see he had gone well past his stop, and knew he was going to publish the book.

- Another editor took the manuscript for Joe McGinniss' *Fatal Vision* on a boating vacation, and got so excited she started editing it — something an editor almost never does until the book is safely signed up.

- A small press editor groaned when he saw David Arora's 680-page mushroom manuscript, then found himself laughing all night at how "witty and well written" it was, and the next day said he'd publish *Mushrooms Demystified*.

- A top agent got the 950-page manuscript of Judith Krantz's *Scruples* on Friday, and by Monday was begging to represent it.

- Frank De Felitta's 725-page manuscript for *Audrey Rose* was read by his editor in two nights — and was under contract within ten days.

Every editor can report similar experiences — or hopes to soon. All editors, says one of them, want that next manuscript "to be the one that will set the heart beating, the adrenaline going, generate the excitement that makes it all worthwhile."

Be it in fiction or nonfiction, Ed is looking for "great reads," "real page-turners," "wow, this is *good*," and other cliches heralding a book that comes alive. Books that are an irresistible read — and writers who take *readers* into account — are very often the ones Ed says "yes" to.

WHY DO PEOPLE READ?

Why do *you* read?

- to be informed or entertained
- to be reassured or comforted or inspired
- to find out who you are or if you're "normal"

- to learn how to live your life better
- to be titillated
- to be persuaded
- to fulfill classroom requirements
- to make sure you're still alive and feeling things
- to identify with successful people
- to live somebody else's life for a while
- to be up on what "everybody else" is reading

Perhaps all these motives can be boiled down to, in Doris Lessing's words: "We read *to find out what is going on.*" This can be taken literally or cosmically, but in the end, reading always seems to derive from human curiosity. Either books satisfy that curiosity, or they get set aside. Books that *continue* satisfying are what we call classics. Or, as Ezra Pound put it: "Literature is news that stays news."

Editors read for the same reasons you do. And when they sign up books, they're "basically responding to their own curiosity about what's happening around them in society," according to editor Fred Hills. "It's that curiosity which will bring an editor, a book idea, and an author together."

Given a supposedly dwindling pool of readers bombarded by a multi-media circus at all times, it sometimes seems that editing books is not the most urgently needed service in the world. The hours are long, the pay is low, the technology is medieval. . . .

But then that book appears that Ed *can't put down*, an experience that keeps many editors reading manuscripts and that helps make editing, in author/editor Toni Morrison's words, "a peculiarly rewarding kind of job."

When editors find a book that comes alive and present it, well edited, to the world, they can allow themselves the luxury of fantasizing that books make a difference.

The migraines of becoming a giant eyeball seem worth it, when book editors can influence whether future generations have "the *People* magazine caption being taught on campus as the preferred literary form," in James Krohe's words. How many other professions are so morally useful?

THE EDITOR AS HUMAN BEING

When editors aren't philosophizing about their jobs, they're reading. They fell into this profession because they love to read.

In a spoof to "prove" that editors *don't* read, agent Richard Curtis once published a minute-by-minute accounting of an editor's day. While "On the Decline of Western Literature" was not wholly kind, the gist of it—there is no time in an editorial office to actually read—is usually true. Manuscripts, especially unsolicited ones, are almost always read on editors' own time, when they'd just as soon be relaxing with family, chatting with friends, working on a tan, or even (sigh) reading for pleasure.

This is why new writers must work harder to capture Ed's full attention than they would to grab a "normal" person, i.e., a reader.

Besides probably being more skilled at skimming, editors don't read too much differently from the way you read. "Almost everyone who reads is an editor," writes editor Saxe Commins, "everyone responds to ideas, has notions of his own about the matter and manner of a book, and is tempted to make revisions as he goes along in accordance with his own background, judgment, prejudices, and critical acumen."

If a book you're reading gets off to a slow start, you're likely to skip around or quit altogether. If you've set a book down and don't feel compelled to pick it up again, you probably won't.

Editors are no different. They begin by paying special attention to your title, your opening sentence, your first few pages.

Editors are looking for something, not that they can always put it into words. Legendary editor Phyllis Grann, who has personally edited some thirty recent bestsellers, claims, "There's something in a manuscript that gets me in the first hundred pages and I can't articulate it. . . . I don't know what it is. I would be afraid to pick one thing, because I'm afraid that I would then start looking for it."

If editors, when they're reading, don't find "it" pretty quickly, they move to the next prospect. "I make my first decision after five minutes of reading," says Sierra Club Books editor Helen Sweetland. Many editors take less.

Just as you frequently read a book on the strength of a friend's recommendation, so is Ed influenced by the first readers of your book—the person who opens the mail, Ed's assistant or secretary, Ed's fellow editors. From the first reader upward, does your book create a buzz of excitement in the office? Is there, in one editor's term, "a wave of house enthusiasm" for your book?

Publishing companies operate by word-of-mouth. "The book comes in and lots of people in the house begin to read it," says editor Kathryn Court, "and that thing happens: Everybody's expectations grow." An especially telling sign is whether Ed has trouble keeping the book in the office—do people keep stealing it to read it?

In fiction, Ed seeks writers who can tell a story. "Books that sell," according to one top editor, "from *War and Peace* to *Gone with the Wind*—they tell a terrific story. And that's a gift." In nonfiction, Ed responds to an allure that *compels* the reader from page to page. Does the book have mounting tension, its own internal logic? Does it offer stepping stones of information the reader can't live without?

Ed's reactions are human ones: First of all, does the book keep Ed awake? Does it make Ed laugh or cry or want to learn something new? Does it make Ed want to skip lunch, dinner, or sex to finish reading it? Is it *about* food or sex?

Oral gratifications and their substitutes are perennial sellers, as are violence, adventure, true crime—"dirty laundry," in the words of a popular song. But cerebral works, like Allan Bloom's *The Closing of the American Mind*, Stephen W. Hawking's *A Brief History of Time*, or Paul Kennedy's *The Rise and Fall of the Great Powers*, can take the bestseller list by surprise, and not all page-turners are melodramas—Garrison Keillor's *Lake Wobegon Days*, Anne Tyler's *Breathing Lessons*, Tom Wolfe's *The Right Stuff*, Isak Dinesen's *Out of Africa*.

Experienced editors, when reading, stay alert to all possibilities that could be published by their companies. They pay attention to their own pulse rate. Are they personally under your spell?

THE EDITOR AS PARENT

Producing a book involves sometimes superhuman labor, all of which rests on Ed's shoulders. In the words of editor Jonathan Galassi: "With the writer the editor is collaborator, psychiatrist, confessor, and amanuensis; in the publishing house he must be politician, diplomat, mediator." Editors will not voluntarily take on these roles for books they don't truly care about.

Ed will act as parent to your book, shepherding it through battles with the editorial board, sessions with the marketing and subrights departments, meetings with production and design departments, struggles to keep the book on schedule, presentation of the book at sales conference, representing it at national and international conventions, making sure it gets publicized and reviewed, fighting for the book when others want to put it out of print, and endless amounts of persuading people to do *things they don't want to do*.

Editors can't publish a book well unless they like it. For editor Thomas Congdon, the deciding factor is "How does the book leave you? Stupefied or stunned or exhausted? . . . The net impact is terribly important. Without that, you don't have anything to build on." Publisher Robert Giroux recalls advice given him by Donald Brace: "A book needs every support it can get and if you, the editor, like it, it starts out with one real friend. . . . And that's a good reason never to take on a book if *you* don't like it."

Ed will be forever collaring disinterested people to read your book: in-house staff, sales reps, librarians and booksellers, friends, reviewers, editors at other companies, perfect strangers. One editor pressed John le Carre's *Little Drummer Girl* manuscript onto a rival editor—and had his own positive opinion of it reinforced. Gary Fisketjon, the newest of the legendary editors, says he "will do almost anything" to get his books read.

For this kind of effort, an editor has to make a real commitment. "Out of the thousands of people in an entire huge publishing empire," writes Donald Westlake in *A Likely Story*, "the only one who cares at all about *your* book is the editor who bought it."

Ed also acts as parent to you. "Editors are parental figures," according to writer Cynthia Ozick, "even when they are much younger than oneself." And if Ed doesn't want to take on this role, Ed rejects the book. Said editor John Farrar of one rejection: "I dislike his manuscripts and don't want to work with him."

Ed will want to feel proud to have signed this book up, and will hate the thought of your book getting sold to another house. Writing copy for the catalog about what a great book this is, Ed plans to believe it.

Editors, like writers, have track records and must work at establishing credibility. The more successful Ed is, the better the future books that get sent Ed's way. The psychic rewards of publishing good books are likely to keep Ed at the same company, where books are used as leverage for more material rewards.

In an ideal world, an editor wants to feel about a book the way Emily Dickinson (whose poems, incidentally, were posthumously rejected by a major publisher who judged them "queer") felt about poetry: "If I feel physically as if the top of my head were taken off, I know that is poetry."

In the real world, such an experience is rare, and if it happened often it would probably prove very stressful. While waiting for such a peak, however, Ed looks for books that come alive.

TRUE STORIES: CATHOLIC GIRLS AND CRANKY NEIGHBORS

It's so crucial to have an alive book that getting a "yes" answer here can sometimes make Ed overlook a "no" answer elsewhere: a lack of previous writing credentials, a large amount of revision required, the apparent absence of a market (Ed might set out to try to *create* a demand for your work).

Several manuscripts that became "my" books came in over the transom—unsolicited, no agents, no prior books published. I was once in charge of a manuscript critique session at a writers' conference, and ended up buying one of the manuscripts I critiqued. (I came away from that conference with four books all told—three from authors who'd published elsewhere but who first approached me there.) That same year, I bought a manuscript that had been written as the first lesson in a correspondence course for writers.

A number of enterprising writers did homework on a fairly obscure series of books, and sent in manuscripts that became part of the series. Several writers researched my company's list and found gaps, which their book proposals filled. Others took heed of the well-publicized news that our list was expanding, and started sending in their best material.

Several writers submitted nonfiction books that I simply could not put down; three of them went on to win awards. An unpublished artist sent in such amusing art samples that we all sat around thinking up plots for her to render—three of which eventually became riotous books.

I met two authors at a poetry conference who sent in manuscripts afterward; some were rejected, but some became books. One author I knew from her superb short stories came to me with ideas for novels, of which three were eventually published and paperback rights sold.

Some authors with reputations in one field wanted to make wild—and well-done—switches to another. Some authors brought old classics to new life with contemporary twists. Others were brimming with outlines and drafts and ideas, never discouraged by seeing many books proposed and few chosen.

Whether unpublished or with a list of credits as long as your arm, all of these writers pulled something off that never ceases to strike me as a miracle: having printed words on a page move me in some way—to laughter, tears, emotion, the satisfaction of seeing private thoughts validated, or the excitement of learning something new. The manuscripts all made their initial impact in *writing*, proving again and again the power of the written word.

Catholic girls, Wisconsin animals, cranky neighbors, the sex life of cats and mice, girl detectives, incest, '60s radicals, lullabies, artificial intelligence, nocturnal sea life—none of these books had all that much in common. Except that, to the question "Does this book come alive?", the answer was always "yes."

HOW TO GET TO THE "YES" ANSWER

Easy to say—"Write a book that comes alive." But how? Even editors themselves can't precisely define "alive." It would seem that you either have a book that springs to life for a particular editor or you don't.

It helps to start from the beginning: your title.

Editors have been known to say "yes" to a book on the strength of a good title alone. Ed may even work with you to make a manuscript live *up* to a good title. Take care with yours:

• Is it catchy, appealing, tantalizing? Even if a title becomes meaningful only within the context of the book—such as *The Color Purple*—it must still intrigue.

• Does your title convey at a glance your subject or thesis? Is your book's "handle" immediately apparent?

• Does it contain words that people like to say? A major magazine once polled its readers, for instance, and found that the three words most likely to grab interest were "love," "lucky," and "let's."

• Is it original? Titles per se can't be copyrighted, but Ed wants to avoid the confusion duplicate titles cause. Check *Books in Print* (more on *BIP* in Question #5) to make sure yours hasn't been used. Does it avoid cliches, such as over-used Biblical or literary references?

• Is it straightforward, memorable, not cryptic?

• Does it stand alone, rather than depending on a subtitle for its meaning? The subtitle, while important to you, will get dropped off along the way when people talk about your book, and in certain important circumstances such as computer listings of upcoming books.

• Is it simple and direct? That's why "How to . . ." and its variations are so popular—they work.

• Is it unambiguous—could your adult title get mistaken for a children's book, your fiction for nonfiction, your serious tome for a humorous book? *Fear of Flying* has virtually passed into the vernacular, but when Erica Jong's book came out, bookstores had it shelved under Aviation, Travel, and Psychology.

• Is it too hard to pronounce? Disappointing sales for James Dickey's *Alnilam* were partly blamed on the book's title. A Little Golden Book called *The Scarebunny* didn't start selling until it was retitled *The Friendly Bunny*. Ed has a hard time going into an editorial meeting with a title that provokes stuttering or snickers.

• If your book is completed, does your title live *up* to your book? Only partly as a joke, I once made an elderly, well-known author ride all the rides at Disneyland until he came up with a great title to match the great book that was already being typeset.

It's better *not* to give Ed a range of possible titles to pick from. Present your best choice—it may not end up as the book's final title, but it is even more important for you now, in selling your book in the first place.

ONCE UPON A TIME

Then there's the all-importance of your opening sentence(s). "First novels begin with a pen," a high-fashion ad declares facetiously—but *good* first novels and first nonfiction books begin with sentences that ignite fires.

Garrison Keillor, creator of the classic first line "It's been a quiet week in Lake Wobegon," says that 95 percent of the world's novels never get written because people can't think of a first line as good as what they *know* will follow. But it's this very challenge that writers working to get published must surmount.

Ed wants to know—posthaste—what you're up to and where you're going. Your first sentence has to induce Ed to go on to the second, and so on, or Ed is not sticking around. The pithy phrases on page 60, the marvelous passage on 140, the triumph of style on 259—they just won't get read.

But wait. Aren't editors being paid to read every word of

your material from first to last? Wrong: Editors are paid to make decisions that can be — and are — made quickly. That's why putting in a page upside-down or transposing pages to test Ed's "thoroughness" is beside the point: Editors do not make money reading books they're going to reject.

A weak first sentence causes Ed to lose trust in you much sooner than you would like. Editor Gordon Lish compares opening a book to accepting a ride: "If you meet someone who shows you he's a bad driver, would you get in the car with him?"

Conversely, by crafting a good first sentence, you're presenting yourself as Ed's alert ally. A slow-starting book will get off to *no* start for people surrounded by twentieth-century temptations. To compete, a book must have a hook — not in the third paragraph or on the fifth page or at the end of a chapter (although these locations are also important), but in the very first sentence.

In college we're taught that a first sentence should contain the entire book in microcosm, the most famous example being F. Scott Fitzgerald's *The Great Gatsby* ("In my younger and more vulnerable years my father gave me some advice that I've been turning over in my mind ever since"). Raymond Carver doesn't start a story until his first line is set, "and then everything seems to radiate out from that line."

Take the time to study first sentences to books you like (a delightful task in itself), and you'll see how the best hooks have rhythm, allure, and that storyteller's voice of electrifying authority. For example:

• Hunter S. Thompson's *Fear and Loathing in Las Vegas*: "We were somewhere around Barstow on the edge of the desert when the drugs began to take hold."

• Lewis Carroll's *Alice in Wonderland*: "Alice was beginning to get very tired of sitting by her sister on the bank and of having nothing to do; once or twice she had peeped into the book her sister was reading, but it had no pictures or conversations in it, 'And what is the use of a book,' thought Alice, 'without pictures or conversation?' "

- Franz Kafka's *The Metamorphosis*: "As Gregor Samsa awoke one morning from uneasy dreams he found himself transformed in his bed into a gigantic insect."

- Jane Austen's *Pride and Prejudice*: "It is a truth universally acknowledged, that a single man in possession of a good fortune must be in want of a wife."

- J.D. Salinger's *The Catcher in the Rye*: "If you really want to hear about it, the first thing you'll probably want to know is where I was born, and what my lousy childhood was like, and how my parents were occupied and all before they had me, but I don't feel like going into it, if you want to know the truth."

- Jack London's *Call of the Wild*: "Buck did not read the newspapers or he would have known that trouble was brewing, not alone for himself, but for every tidewater dog strong of muscle and with warm, long hair, from Puget Sound to San Diego."

Experiment with starting your book *in media res* — in the middle of things, not at the proper sequential beginning. Ann Beattie's editor supposedly lopped off her stories' first pages, which had a radical effect on her first sentences. One *New Yorker* editor routinely cuts the first two or three paragraphs of any article.

A good book calls for a first line that's an invitation to adventure, a chance to learn and grow, an opportunity to enter an intriguing new world — and a hook to keep Ed reading onward to signing up your book.

WHAT ABOUT THE REST OF THE BOOK?

Also important are all chapter beginnings and endings. Chapter endings call for hooks to keep drawing the reader on. These can be dramatic (as in mysteries) or more subtle (as in nonfiction), but they're always necessary to keep forcing the reader to keep turning those pages.

Concentrate on the momentum of your writing. In nonfiction, build one paragraph or chapter upon the other in logical sequences allowing for no useless digressions. In fiction, never let your tension slacken. Even the simplest of books requires a snappy pace. Says children's author Maurice Sendak: "You have to put a little motor in so as to ease and tempt the child into 'gotta go on, gotta go on'. . . . You must disguise the fact that there is a dead pause because you have to turn that page."

(For writers who *aren't* children's book writers, an excellent starting place for studying what makes books come alive is the best of current books for children, which are scrupulously written and edited with this very factor in mind.)

Analyze the tone of your writing. Is it what you need—conversational? academic? comic? storytelling? ironic? hortatory?—to make your material accessible to the audience you're trying to reach?

Consistency of tone is important, as is consistency in general. If your heroine flashes green eyes on page 2 and brown eyes on page 12, if your hero's personality changes from one page to the next with no explanation, if you assert one thing on page 10 and its apparent opposite in the next chapter, Ed loses confidence in you. Unless you make the world of your book real and complete and consistent, you won't make Ed suspend disbelief in it.

If you include a fact that is clearly false or out-of-date, editors assume you mean for them to do your research for you—and will read no further. Unfair as it may seem, one inaccuracy or misjudgment throws the entirety into doubt—even parts on which you have worked very hard.

THE CAUSES OF DEAD WRITING

It helps to keep the human factor in mind at all times. What is the effect you intend—to distract, to inform, to titillate, to inspire, to change lives, to amuse, to persuade, or what? Write *for a reader*, not merely to display your intelligence on the page. Self-expression may be good for the soul, but it's not what Ed seeks.

It's amazing how picturing your audience can clean up your writing. It will enable you to spot, for example, contradictions between two equally beloved paragraphs, and you will realize that one of them has got to go. You may see, in fiction, how you've stayed so true to life that you've tripped yourself up with unbelievable coincidences and other lapses in logic. Real life is not always believable—it's the writer's job to make it so.

Picturing a reader will also help you to develop your own voice, another characteristic of an alive book. What exactly is it you're trying to say, and to whom? Why are you uniquely qualified to say it? Lively writing is a by-product of answering these questions.

With fiction, it's the writing, not the bare bones of the plot (and *not* talking about it) that contains the life of your book. If E. B. White had called up his editor and said, "How about a novel about the relationship between a pig and spider?" she would have replied, "Thanks, but no thanks," and the world would have lost *Charlotte's Web* (and its knockout first sentence: " 'Where's Papa going with that ax?' said Fern to her mother as they were setting the table for breakfast").

Study current "page-turners"—your favorites and/or the ones on the bestseller lists. What makes these books work (or not work) for you? What makes them tick?

In the end, however, what makes a book come alive is not imitation of other books. It's the passion you feel about *your* book. Have an honest talk with yourself: Does your book move *you*? Are *you* emotionally involved with it and passionate about it? If so, this will come across on the page.

Conversely, writing a book you think the editor wants, or what the market wants and you think it deserves, will deaden your writing. Ed notices when you underestimate your reader, and can spot a patronizing or didactic attitude a mile away.

The only method for writing a book that comes alive is to write what you feel deeply about. "The true writer always plays to an audience of one," according to *Elements of Style*. Two small press editors agree: "Made-to-order books are never nearly as good as those that spring from passion and experience."

EDITORS IN LOVE

Editors will know a lively book "when they see it," so there's little point in writing merely to please them. Editors aren't *you*. They simply can't *conceive* of all the wonderful things you're capable of. They're only qualified to say, "Now, that is wonderful," *after* the fact.

Many stated reasons for rejection are in fact euphemisms for an editor's not falling in love with your book. This sort of rejection is no more pleasant to receive than any other, but when you can read between the lines, it does connote hope: You don't necessarily have a failed book, but rather a need to keep trying until you connect with the editor who *does* fall in love.

3.

DOES THE BOOK HAVE A CLEARLY DEFINED FOCUS?

I often think how shocked authors
would be if they listened to the salesmen
selling their books. They've worked a
year on their book — two years, three
years, maybe longer. And there it is. A
word or two and a decision is made.
— Bruce Bliven,
quoting book salesman George Scheer

The vast majority of writers, as everyone knows, never get on talk shows to give potential readers the message of their books. Instead, a succession of third parties performs this job for them:

- editors, who use an average of four minutes per book in pitching their seasonal list to sales managers at sales conference time
- sales managers, who use an average of two minutes per book in explaining each book to the traveling sales reps
- traveling sales reps, who use an average of *30 seconds* per book in selling your book to bookstores

Such is the reality of publishing, wherein books are bought and sold on the basis of sentences.

In order for a decision to be made, your book *must* have a clearly defined focus. "Only when you have gone on a sales call with a company sales rep," says author Leonard Felder, "will you know how hard it is to sell fifty titles in fifteen minutes and how important it is to have a clear focus for your book."

Ed may like your writing, may even think you have a spark of a good idea, but an immediate perception that your idea is unfocused will seem a ready excuse for rejection. Frankly, editors are looking for a reason to reject books. They're swamped with books they've already acquired, and they know the odds against finding something publishable in that week's stack.

Ed cannot afford to launch an unfocused idea into a marketplace teeming with focused ideas. Editors recognize focus almost by instinct, and are usually generalists: They know a little about a lot of things. The life cycle of an editor, according to editor Rust Hills, "requires infinite flexibility and a sort of superior-grade butterfly mind." The same criteria for a clear focus apply whether it's an autobiographical novel or a car-repair guide.

From the moment Ed opens your package, Ed is looking for your book's handle. What are you promising to do? Can it be summed up in one sentence? A sentence that Ed can use:

- in persuading the editorial board to back the decision to buy the book
- in obtaining an appropriate design from the art department
- in filling out forms such as your book contract
- in capturing the attention of sales reps and booksellers
- in succinctly pitching the book to the sub-rights staff
- in giving future buyers the key to spreading the all-important word of mouth about your book

Ed isn't the only one who's overworked—all of these people have a universe of books competing for their time and attention. To get your share, you must, in the words of John Boswell in *The Awful Truth About Publishing*, make your book "publisher proof": "If you can shape and focus an idea for a book that readers want to buy, then the publisher will probably want to buy it from you, and the bookseller will probably want to buy it from the publisher."

TAKING PICTURES

"Focus," a term usually encountered in photography, is indeed the right metaphor for evaluating your book.

Take a mental picture of your manuscript or proposal. Does the picture make a strong statement? Or are the edges blurry, the outlines ill-defined—does one theme or message tend to merge into another? Is the whole picture balanced? Is attention centered on the picture's real subject? Or are unimportant details cluttering up the whole? What is your perspective, and is it consistent, interesting, and appropriate? How could you alter the picture to make it more focused and say what you really mean to say even better? What would you delete or augment?

Ed looks for evidence that you're aware of the need for focus:

- If your book is fiction, can you tell a story that keeps up the tension?
- If you have a nonfiction book, does it contain a pervasive thread of argument?
- Does every sentence tend to contribute to the whole? Or do you get off the track with useless digressions?
- Do you have a thesis, a definite and consistent point of view?
- Have you let the thesis overwhelm your material, making it preachy or didactic? Are you distracted by a "message," ignoring character or plot? Are you writing a lecture rather than a book?
- Does the focus jump around? Do you start off by concentrating on one theme or subject, and then go off on tangents, perhaps never getting back to your original premise?

An erratic focus is liable to irritate Ed, who will feel misled and cheated—not a favorable disposition for looking beyond this flaw to the possible *merits* of your book.

Meandering books usually don't sell, either. Harry Hoffman, an authority on what sells, by virtue of being head of the Waldenbooks chain, says, "People want something short that they can read in a night." Not all good books are short, of course, but the point is that contemporary readers lose patience with unfocused books, no matter how good they may be in other respects.

Keeping in mind that we read *to find out what is going on*, there is a need, in writer Joseph Brodsky's words, "for concision, condensation, fusion — for [books] that bring the human predicament, in all its diversity, into its sharpest possible focus."

The question of focus — what you promise — applies to fiction and nonfiction equally. No less a writer than John Steinbeck felt that novelists should be able to state their themes in one sentence. Some novels that appear diffuse are actually focused very tightly. Two huge novels that take place entirely within twenty-four hours, for example, are *Under the Volcano* by Malcolm Lowry and *Ulysses* by James Joyce (whose first book, *Dubliners*, was rejected by twenty-two publishers, incidentally).

And the answer to this question is almost more important than whether or not you *deliver* what you promise. If Ed is excited enough by a cleverly focused idea, Ed can actually help you fine-tune the book.

In the back of Ed's mind are pictures of books that sell — does yours fit the template or not?

"How-to" books are one example: The focus is explicit in the very title. Good "whodunit's" are another — a riveting book such as Scott Turow's *Presumed Innocent* is tightly focused from first page to last. Lurid true crime stories of the rich and nasty are another. These, in editor Larry Ashmead's words, are "an editor's dream. . . . They're exciting books to write for the writers, to edit for the editors, for the publisher to publish, and for the salesmen to sell." They have a niche, whereas the *lack* of a niche frequently supplies the excuse for poor sales of any given book.

It *is* possible to go too far in the other direction, making a book *too* focused, too limited. Ed will sometimes reject a book for this reason — not always astutely: *The Complete Book of Running* by James Fixx was rejected by one major publisher — "A whole book on running?" — only to sell more than 2 million copies for another.

But it is useful to contemplate this reaction and counter it if need be. Analyzing your own focus *before* sending out your material will benefit you in defending your book to Ed and, in the case of rejection, future Eds.

Like Fixx, you must remain confident in your book despite rejection, and confidence comes in large part from having thought through your book's focus yourself.

Ideally, focus is part of your writerly life. You must, just to keep creating and not get discouraged in the face of rejection, keep *yourself* focused. "So much bitterness exists between writers and their publishers," says writer John Irving. "You have to eliminate the distractions. You've got to keep focused."

TRUE STORY: RECIPE FOR AN UNFOCUSED BOOK

The first proposal for the book you're holding in your hands, which at the time was titled *What Editors Look For*, went exactly like this:

1. Brief overview of publishing
   a. Different types of publishing
   b. The publishing process from idea to finished book
   c. How the editor fits in
2. The typical editor's day [an endless list of tasks]
3. Who are these editors?
   a. Backgrounds, personalities, and training
   b. Types of editors
   c. Editorial hierarchy in the publishing company
4. How editors find manuscripts, Part 1: Opening their mail
5. What turns an editor on and off [endless lists]
6. What goes into a typical reader's report on a manuscript
7. How editors find manuscripts, Part 2: Books generated by editors [an endless list of where editors get their ideas]
8. How final decisions are made
9. What writers can do to make sure their manuscripts stand out [conclusion, bibliography, etc.]

This first proposal, with its utter lack of focus, would have gotten me nowhere fast. Not until Chapter 9 — out of nine chapters! — did I get to the point.

Sure enough, by the time the second outline was accepted, "more tightly focused" were the editor's very words.

I think what editors do all day is terribly fascinating; perhaps ten editors besides myself would pick up a book called

Lifestyles of the Editors. You would just as soon cut the froufrou and find out the keys to getting Ed to buy your book. There is (covertly) a great deal of information *about* editors in the current book, but the focus has changed radically: It's now on what the reader wants to know—keys you can actually use.

THREE SUGGESTIONS

One moral to be learned from this story is that it's a useful exercise to write down, in outline form, *everything* you'd like to say. For me, a long-winded effort was necessary in order to focus on what I needed to prune.

Do this *before* you send your material to Ed, who will be grateful. A well-known author once sent me an outline that was a small book in itself; rigorous pruning eventually unearthed the fascinating book inside. Overly ambitious outlines, common even among established authors, can, for the new writer, make it more difficult to get published in the first place.

A second lesson is that, even if you've hit upon the all-important good idea (to answer Question #1), your work may not be over yet: Before you can sell your good idea, you may need to bring down the focus to one or two elements of the idea.

Normally, editors can't do this work for you. They don't have the time, and also they're not *you*. It's *your* idea, and often, the only one qualified to focus it is you.

The third and most important point to highlight is that, in checking the focus on your idea, it helps, as usual, to focus your idea to a *reader*.

HOW TO GET TO THE "YES" ANSWER

Besides the tips above, think about how you spread word of mouth to friends on books you like. What terms do you use, what comparisons? Do you say, "It's like [title of book everyone knows and loves], but with [a significant difference or advantage]?" "It's a new twist on [tried-and-true theme or subject]?" "It's a really original [something] you *gotta* read?" Do you sum up the plot, marvel at the language, rave about what you've learned?

All of these are similar terms to what an editor will use in describing the focus of your book. Help the editor out here by doing it yourself—in your cover letter, preferably in your very first sentence. Often, Ed may end up referring to the book forevermore by using the very same terms you do.

Try out the exercise of describing your book in a single sentence. Can you do it without resorting to sixteen clauses? How do you sum up your book to your friends and relatives? Do they grasp your concept right away, or do you find yourself adding a lot of explanation and qualifiers?

If you're having trouble editing your idea to a single sentence, write a letter to your target editor. Make it as long as you like—pages if necessary—explaining what you are trying to do and why. Justify, clarify, proselytize, defend, scream: Get everything down on paper. Then conclude by boiling it all down to one (1) sentence. Put the letter in your file, and put the sentence in the cover letter you actually send.

What focus or twist can you give so that your potential readers will see your book as a *must-have*? The time you spent on your title will pay off here—you should be able to use it to display your focus.

Experiment with changing your focus. Can you enlarge the focus to make an otherwise esoteric book address a larger group of readers? More often, narrowing the focus of your book may paradoxically increase the number of people who will actually buy it. Narrowing your focus can improve your writing as well, and make your book better overall. "The most important lesson in the writing trade," says Robert Heinlein, is "that any manuscript is improved if you cut away the fat."

GETTING INTIMATE

Think in terms of a reader—not just a reader predisposed to you, but a tough consumer: a stranger you want to spend $20 (or the average price for the type of book you're writing) on your idea. Is your idea worth $20? How can you focus it to make it seem worth that and more?

Get on intimate terms with your intended audience. Inspect the bookstore nearest you, or the type of store most likely to carry the book you're working on. Inhale the atmosphere. How is the store organized and what are the categories? How are books displayed that seem to fit *no* category? Study the tried-and-true sellers. Study what books appeal to *you* and why. What attracts you to certain categories, to certain books? Where would your book be placed in the store?

"The savvy aspiring author," writes John Boswell, "can figure out more from snooping around [the local bookstore] than from reading fifty books on publishing." (Especially books called *What an Editor Does All Day*.)

Also, by researching your competition (more on this in Question #5), you'll get ideas and see ways to focus your book to make it stand out, proving to yourself that your slant is best.

KEEPING READERS ON THE PATH

What is your destination, or the *target* of your book? Many writers, especially mystery writers, actually write the endings to their books *first*. Your ending may prove a useful starting point in fine-tuning your focus.

It helps to outline your book or map it out thoroughly, organizing your material so that it's as clear and accessible as you can make it. If you digest and focus your facts before including them, you'll save yourself future embarrassment. Analyze your idea from all sides. Does each chapter or part contribute to the whole? What could get cut? What needs beefing up?

Do you keep your destination in view? "Readers are like sheep," editor John Wood quotes a professor of his as saying — "if there's any gate on the right or left, they'll take it. You must, therefore, always keep them on the path."

Outlining your book puts you well on the way to putting

together your book proposal, and an estimated 75 percent of all trade (bookstore) books sold to editors today are sold on the basis of proposals, not completed manuscripts. For fiction, a proposal consists of the first three (*not* any three) chapters and a plot synopsis. For nonfiction, a proposal includes a chapter-by-chapter outline, a sample piece of writing or a list of your credits, and a letter explaining your book, its market and competition, why you're the perfect person to write it, and when you can deliver the manuscript.

Putting a focused proposal together is, believe it or not, largely a matter of common sense, if you know a little about book publishing (from market research as outlined here and from learning to temporarily think like an editor). Essentially, include what Ed needs to make a decision and not a word more. There are also whole books on this very topic—see the Bibliography.

The very act of putting together your proposal will, ideally, make you think your material through so thoroughly that by the time it's done, whatever was mushy has become focused—and eminently salable.

4.

DOES THE BOOK HAVE A CLEARLY DEFINED AUDIENCE?

*In literature, as in love, we are aston-
ished at what is chosen by others.*
                    — André Maurois

Suppose your target editor says, "This is a good book. . . ." Hur-
ray! "But"—uh oh—"hard as I try, I cannot imagine who would
buy it." What happens next?

Depending on the strength of Ed's answers to the previous
three questions, Ed may make a leap of faith and side with
Maurois: There *are* people who will choose this book, even
though Ed can't readily picture them at the moment.

Sometimes editors will like a book so much that they'll forc-
ibly "create" an audience for it. Says editor Bill Whitehead:
"First I want to know if the idea—nonfiction—or the theme—
fiction—*works* for me. . . . *Then*, and only then, I'll say to myself,
'I'd love to find a market for this title, and if I can't, by God,
we'll have to *create* one.' " Another top commercial editor agrees:
"I think every now and then you can decide to teach the public
that there's a book they need to read that they didn't realize
they needed to read."

On the other hand, Ed may take the easy way out and return the book with the suggestion that you try a more specialized publisher. As in love with your book as Ed may be, Ed
will be realistic about justifying it to a devil's advocate editorial
board.

Writers can avoid this reason for rejection by demonstrating to Ed what audience they're writing for—even quantifying it when necessary.

Really savvy writers research the typical first printings of their sort of book. For example, first printings of typical hardcover books range from 3,000 to 10,000. Generally, it's uneconomical to print less than a yearly quantity of 5,000 copies of a book. (A new book selling less than 5,000 a year loses money for the publisher, due to high production costs per book.)

Ed wants to feel confident that you've got a readily identifiable audience of *at least* 5,000 people a year who buy books and are likely to buy yours in particular. An editor is gambling, says publisher David Godine, "that there are five thousand souls with tastes as benighted and backward as yours out there who will plunk down their [money]." With a commercial book, according to John Boswell, "If your potential audience is less than two to three million, reaching them through bookstores becomes problematic." After all, Harold Robbins's books have been known to sell as many as 22,000 copies *a day*.

Assuming you're not Harold Robbins, Ed will be asking some hard questions:

- Exactly who will buy your book?
- What sex, what age level, what interest group, what literacy rate?
- Is it a bookstore book or an institutional (school and library) book? Or does it fall between the cracks?
- Will it appeal to people who typically buy books?
- Is the audience you're writing for large enough to justify the expense and energy of publishing your book?
- Can the book be shaped to meet the needs of a larger audience?
- Does your book fit in with the identity of that house? Will it appeal to the same audience the house has successfully sold to in the past, or an audience the house has been wanting to reach?

The audience for a book is not always clear. Editorial board deliberations over ambiguous cases—where "the subject matter is interesting but has a less clearly defined readership," as editor

Michael Korda puts it—can take "hours, days even." An audience might exist for your work—but will this audience *buy* it?

Ed, as an entrepreneurial risk-taker within a publishing company, is constantly making a judgment here. As in all risk-taking, a little bit of irrationality is involved. Editors launch a new book, writes editor Peter Davison, "the way a poet launches a poem or a spider launches a web—into the void, across the abyss that separates one reader perusing a text in a room from another reading the same book a thousand miles or years away."

On the verge of accepting a book, Ed is not all that different from the way Frederick Barthelme describes writers: "You're still out in the middle of nowhere doing something nobody asked you to do, and you suspect, all polite evidence to the contrary, that they didn't ask because they don't want, and if they did want, they'd get it elsewhere."

For writers, the remedy here is to picture your audience, and the same is true for editors. "To acquire a book without a perception of the market and how to reach that market," says editor Susan Moldow, "is a disservice to the author . . . and the publisher."

Estimating the size of the audience is something editors instinctively learn to do even as they first examine your material. Generally, says editor Pat Strachan, "an editor will have enough experience publishing books so that the potential audience is in the back of his or her mind all the time—it's part of an editor's natural thought processes."

Over time, editors develop theories, even biases, about what books sell to what audiences. "An editor's only permanent alliance is with the audience," writes editor Arthur Plotnik. "Authors know their subject. Editors specialize in knowing the audience." Editors are paid to know their audiences better than writers do—but writers have access to much of the same information.

WHO BUYS BOOKS?

And now for some truly useful statistics about the audiences for books you might be writing:

If you write fiction, for instance, did you know that an estimated 70 percent of all fiction is bought by women? Bestselling novelists Judith Barnard and Michael Fain (in a turnabout from centuries past) deliberately write under a female name, Judith Michael, to capitalize on this fact. "There's a big market there — light reading for intelligent ladies," claims bestselling writer Rosamunde Pilcher. In romance fiction, women account for close to 100 percent of sales (and they also supposedly make love 74 percent more often than women who *don't* buy romances!).

Women buy more books in general. Says one Chicago bookseller: "I can think of more things that women read that men don't than the other way around. I can't think of anything that men read that women don't."

If you're having trouble selling your fiction, have you considered switching to nonfiction, which accounts for half of books sold (except in children's books, where fiction accounts for more like 70 percent)?

Did you know it's believed that most hardcover novels are bought to be given as gifts?

That horror books are bought primarily by teenage boys — and the same women who buy romances?

That science fiction readers are mostly males under 21, with the largest market in northern California?

That regional books make a very tough sell to a New York publisher, who would rather sell 200 copies of a book in each state than 10,000 in one state only? That New York editors are highly prejudiced toward topics that appeal to fellow Manhattanites? A major New York editor once said, only half-joking, that she wouldn't offer a contract unless a book appealed to her upper-middle-class friends on the Upper West Side. (Solution here: Think small — see next section.)

That, until recently, the majority (85 percent) of children's books were bought by institutions (schools and libraries), but that the figure is now 50 percent, with the other half sold in bookstores primarily to women between the ages of twenty-five and forty-nine, who tend to look for the books *they* read as children?

Do you know which book audiences regenerate themselves (e.g., a new generation of children's book readers is born every few years; the market for job-hunting guides or atlases continually regenerates)?

Just because the potential audience for a topic is large does not mean these people will automatically buy books on that topic. Editors know that a majority of the population never enters a bookstore—estimates run as high as 80 percent. Indeed, 20 percent of American adults are estimated to be functionally illiterate, which means that books on topics that might appeal to this audience are not going to sell, period.

Sports such as auto racing are enormously popular, for example, but books on auto racing don't sell. The many fans of actress Vanna White "want to look, not read," comments one bookseller—hence, poor sales for *Vanna Speaks*. Collections of short stories were previously thought to have no audience, until the current boom, inspired perhaps by the reading habits of a generation raised on half-hour TV shows.

Clues as to who buys books can be found in any bookstore. Gardeners buy books—notice the plethora of gardening books. The same is true of enthusiasts of cooking (cookbooks account for one in twenty of all nonfiction purchases, and one-third of the buyers are men), home decorating and improvement, military history, economics (or just plain money), dance, and such "New Age" topics as astrology, self-healing, psychology, and mysticism. Topics of interest to forty-five- to fifty-four-year-olds (where the highest population growth is occurring) are plentiful.

The largest section in many stores now is the children's book section, the biggest growth area in trade books. People who buy computers also buy books. (In fact, one out of every five nonfiction sales fits the category of "reference/instruction/computer books," with men the larger proportion of buyers.) People who go to movies buy books. College students buy books, and so do their professors. Writers buy books, as do editors and publishing people, as do people who *want* to write books.

"Category" fiction has a built-in audience—be it fans of romance, science fiction, horror, westerns, mysteries, male action, or pornography. "The known factor of a preexisting audience," writes SF editor David Hartwell, "guarantees a certain minimal level of success for books appropriately placed." According to

Mary Higgins Clark, "Mystery suspense is the most popular genre in the world."

Then there are diet and fitness books, which currently account for *9 percent of all hardcover sales*. At any given time, 10 percent of the population is seriously dieting, and the market for diet books continually regenerates itself, since 97 percent of people who lose weight gain it back within a year. This audience looks endlessly for new and easy ways to lose weight, with publishers endlessly ready to fulfill that need.

THINK SMALL: A VALUABLE ESCAPE HATCH

Editors who don't sign up diet books, or anything so obviously commercial, are frequently to be found at regional publishers, small presses, and university presses—the "more specialized companies" that larger houses are referring to when they suggest other homes for your book.

For the new writer, all indications are that your chances of being published by a small press are significantly greater than your chances of getting a contract from a major commercial New York publisher.

How to connect with the right small press for you? Start by researching listings in the annually revised *International Directory of Little Magazines and Small Presses* (forty pages when it began in 1965, now 850 pages), as well as in the annually revised *Writer's Market* and *Novel & Short Story Writer's Market*. Small presses can be found in every state, especially around San Francisco, New York City, and in Iowa, Texas, the Northwest, the Northeast, and the Southwest.

Out of all publishers in the United States, a majority (between 14,000 and 20,000) are small presses that account for nearly 50 percent of the sales volume of all books published, and *more* than 50 percent of the titles in print. A small press can be a one-book company, or else too ephemeral for you to consider, but many of them are actively seeking good books of the riskier, more esoteric variety.

Some small presses are more profit-oriented than others.

"I'm not trying to compromise my integrity," says one California alternative press editor, "but I'll be damned if I'm going to publish books that people aren't going to *buy*. . . . We're going to publish things we like, but readers have to want them." Agrees another editor: "I like a business that thrives."

Other small press editors respond more idiosyncratically. Susan Hunter of Susan Hunter Publishing (a small Atlanta publisher) wants books that she's proud to put her name on. For some small presses, potential profit may not even be the major consideration, but rather your basic viewpoint (with feminist, regional, radical, or black small presses, for example) or your book's literary merit (with many university presses).

Because they *are* small, small presses are often willing to experiment in ways the larger houses can no longer afford to do. "Books that larger houses consider too risky . . . too feminist, too gay or lesbian, too political, or simply too literary," says small press editor Faith Conlon, "are precisely the books small presses are publishing successfully." Many small presses aggressively market their tightly focused nonfiction titles through nontraditional, nonbookstore outlets.

A small press will generally print in smaller quantities (though *What Color Is Your Parachute?* and other books have evolved into genuine bestsellers), but what it does print, it tries very hard to *sell*.

Agents as well as authors are hailing the small press in an age when New York publishers are consolidating into ever-larger behemoths. One top agent is delighted to see good small presses becoming a new force in publishing, "scouting for new and different authors, and publishing literature." Says another agent: "Much as in the motion picture industry, smaller companies will spring up acting as independent producers for the major houses." According to a top commercial editor, at small presses authors are never "mid-list. They *are* the list."

An additional, very important alternative to large commercial houses is the rise of university presses (publishers associated with specific universities), which previously published only serious scholarly nonfiction books. Now many — not all — university presses are publishing contemporary fiction for audiences too obscure to attract the attention of a large publisher. Advances are low to nonexistent and the sales are generally lower than a large house's, but university presses know their audience well and keep books in print longer than most larger houses. Research these presses as carefully as you would any publisher, by checking the listings in the directories listed above.

All editors at all publishing companies, however, will ask the same question about what audience you're writing for. "An editor's primary function," says publisher Sol Stein, "is to help the writer realize that he must keep the audience in mind while writing: in fiction, with a view toward moving that audience as often as possible; in nonfiction, toward getting that audience to accept what the writer has written as accurate, true, and, if possible, wise."

Small presses will not necessarily present the most lucrative opportunity for you, but they're currently a wide-open market for manuscripts, a valuable escape hatch for writers who find themselves stifled.

By doing your own research, you can get your book to the publisher who is most likely to see the same potential audience as you do and who publishes for that audience.

HOW TO GET TO THE "YES" ANSWER

The single most important tip here is to research the publishers you send your book to, because you will at the same time be researching your audience.

The average consumer couldn't care less what publishers' names are on the spines of books. But you, as a writer who wants to publish, must become a scholar of the publishers you want to work with. There are many audiences—choose your publishers carefully.

Are the publishers you're considering successful with your kind of book? Are they expanding their list or cutting back? Do they do a good job of reaching their audience—are their books in the stores you'd expect to find them in, or is it a struggle to find them? "What is important," stresses consultant Leonard

Shatzkin, "is that the author find out, before he negotiates a contract, before he even submits a manuscript or an outline, the strengths and weaknesses of the publisher."

You can find this kind of information by:

- getting a subscription to *Publishers Weekly*, the weekly trade magazine. It's not cheap, but it's your single best source for up-to-date information on publishers. Most editors and many writers are *PW* addicts. Most libraries carry *PW* behind the desk and will let you see it if you ask.
- researching bookstores and libraries to learn who publishes what and what's been done. Watch the customers: Who are they and what are they buying? Who *publishes* what they're buying? What percentage of bookstore space is given to the type of book you're writing?
- interviewing booksellers. You'll gain some strong opinions about publishers.
- studying directories such as *Writer's Market* and noting carefully what things individual publishers want to see and what things they don't.
- buying the annual "publishers round-up" issues of *Writer's Digest* and *The Writer*, which describe what's happening with each publisher.
- joining writers' organizations and scrutinizing their newsletters for publisher information.
- obtaining publishers' current catalogs listing all upcoming books. Call the sales departments and ask to have a catalog mailed to you.
- attending conventions in your area where publishers will have booths exhibiting new books and catalogs.

A day at a convention can net you a wealth of information and a shopping bag of useful catalogs. If you know or are a 1) bookseller, 2) librarian, or 3) teacher, you can find out the locales and times of the next national or regional conventions of 1) the American Booksellers Association, 2) the American Library Association, and 3) the International Reading Association, for primary school teachers, or National Council of Teachers of English, for secondary school teachers.

Research on publishers will *always* pay off. Many editors

frown upon multiple manuscript submissions, for example, because these usually do not show any of this kind of research on the part of the writer. The writer has no conception of what audience the publisher publishes for.

"To publish a book is to more than just print and distribute it," says publisher Howard Kaminsky. "Publishing is trying to find an audience for a book." And *getting* published is trying to find the publisher most likely to respond to what you're doing.

THE VALUE OF STATISTICS

It's a useful exercise to spend time picturing the audience for your book. If *you* have trouble envisioning your audience, it's a good bet Ed will also. No less a writer than John Updike carries a mental picture of his audience: "When I write, I aim in my mind not toward New York but toward a vague spot a little east of Kansas. I think of the books on library shelves . . . and a countryish teen-aged boy finding them, and having them speak to him."

Editors deciding whether or not to accept a book need evidence that you know who you're writing for. So much the better if you can provide statistics on numbers of potential readers, especially when they're statistics Ed would have to look up anyway. If you're writing a book on AIDS, for example, tell Ed the latest AIDS statistics as they apply to the potential audience for your book. The same is true for any problem—balding men, abused children, women who read too much—or a situation that affects a quantifiable segment of the population.

Keep your eyes and ears open for statistics and results of surveys all around you that you can use to define your audience—in magazines, newspapers, TV documentaries and news shows, other books.

Investigate the reference department of your library for useful books such as the *Encyclopedia of Associations* (groups to which you can write for information), the *Directory of Directories* (to find out which books will help you), and the annual *Statistical Abstract of the United States* and other books of statistics. Librarians will usually be eager to help.

Use these statistics to support your own writing, or to get new ideas. "The greatest joy and the highest privilege of a creative editor," writes publisher M. Lincoln Schuster, "is to touch life at all points and discover needs *still unmet*—and find the best authors to meet them." Writers who publish don't wait for editors to find them—they research unmet needs and meet them themselves.

In your letter to Ed, it helps to make astute comparisons between your book and other books, especially successful ones (and *ideally* ones the publisher has published or that your target editors edited). Place your book on a continuum. Ed will pick up the connection and grasp immediately what audience you're talking about without your necessarily having to quantify it.

WHAT DO YOU THINK OF YOUR AUDIENCE?

Once you've identified your audience, it's important to respect it. "No one can write decently who is distrustful of the reader's intelligence, or whose attitude is patronizing," according to E. B. White. The phenomenon of writers writing down to their audience is especially common with children's book manuscripts, but is frequent in all fields.

"Neither editing or writing . . . any kind of fiction," writes mystery editor Hope Dellon, "can be undertaken cynically—'I hate this sort of thing, but the morons out there should like it'— with much hope of success." Part of an editor's job is to make sure the audience gets treated respectfully. "Novelists sometimes think of their audiences as subordinates being exposed to what is good for them," says one commercial editor. "My role as editor is to disabuse them."

Don't patronize your audience, but don't confuse them, either. You can check this out by soliciting opinions from readers you trust and who read your type of book. Editors love material that's appropriate to the target audience. "A good editor is a reader's advocate," say two top editors, and if Ed can't understand part or all of a book, Ed's going to assume it's over the audience's head as well.

Take care to avoid getting asked the favorite question of Harold Ross, *The New Yorker*'s late editor: "What the hell do you mean?"

It also helps to respect the genre you're writing in. In your effort to put your own stamp on it, don't ignore the established conventions of that genre — or you'll alienate your core audience of loyal buyers.

"The best advice that one can give a writer," says editor Page Cuddy, "is not to condescend to the genre or try to pack a literary idea into a more commercial form in hopes of selling it."

ENLARGING THE AUDIENCE

Can you think of ways to re-orient your material to make it appeal to a larger percentage of buyers? If you're writing a book for working mothers, would it make sense to enlarge your audience to include all working people? Conversely, if you're writing a book for writers, would it make sense to narrow your focus to beginning writers? The potential audience is smaller, but the more specific focus is more likely to make *buyers* out of that audience.

Rather than writing the story of your life, can you twist it to make it more universal? This technique works even for celebrities (whose unadorned life stories publishers would be likely to buy): Bill Cosby on fatherhood and middle age; Donald Trump on making deals; Suzanne Somers on children of alcoholics; Elizabeth Taylor on women's attitudes toward weight.

Interview a bookseller about what's selling and what the prospects for a book like yours would be. Ed does this all the time, and doing your own footwork here can only help you.

Writers may even want to experience what's considered the ideal education for an editor: working a stint as a clerk in a bookstore. It's by far the most direct way to see firsthand who the buyers of books are and what they do and don't read.

THE MOST IMPORTANT
AUDIENCE

The traditional advice in determining your audience is to start with yourself. "If you capture what you *feel*," says editor Charlotte Zolotow, "the writing will find its own audience later."

Write about what you care about deeply—this is what the editor looks for. "Too many people, adults and children alike, do not know what they want until they see it or have experienced it," writes children's book editor Jean Karl. This makes the job of editors to "not only pick what sells but to sell what we believe is good."

And this makes the job of writers to write the best book they can, out of their own passion. Intuition will lead them on from there to an audience of editors eager to see more.

5.

IS THE BOOK ORIGINAL AND FRESH?

Your manuscript is both good and orig-
inal; but the part that is good is not
original, and the part that is original
is not good.
                    — Samuel Johnson

In a frequently anthologized mystery story, "The Mother Goose Madman" by Betty Ren Wright, a literary psychopath terrorizes a children's book editor by, among other chilling tactics, enclosing a live deadly spider in with his latest manuscript submission.

No need to get drastic—but Ed *will* be looking for compelling evidence (of the more traditional sort) that a book is original and fresh.

Editors seldom feel more deflated than when, after having gotten excited about a project, they learn via research (or are told by the editorial board) that "it's already been done." Such a book usually gets a quick rejection.

To avoid this frustration, Ed wants to know:

• Do you have something new to say? Or have you picked a topic that's been rehashed many times, or a fad for which the market will be glutted by the time your book sees the light of day?

• Do you have a new wrinkle on a subject of perennial interest? Or does your plot have whiskers?

• Are all your facts and research up-to-date?

61

- Have you contributed something fresh to the field you've chosen?

- Is your topic enlivened with a sense of humor or wit?

- If your book seems timely or topical now, will it still seem so a year down the road? Ed thinks nine to eighteen months into the future — which is the average length of time a book takes from manuscript to bound book. Is your subject already dated, likely to get dated quickly, or so timely that sales would drop to zero a few months after publication?

- If your book capitalizes on current or upcoming events, does Ed have the capacity to publish it in time? Some publishers are equipped to publish books faster than nine to eighteen months (even "instantly," with burning issues of the day), whereas others take their time in producing volumes "for the ages." (You can tell which is which by noticing how current the information is in the books you read, and any bookseller can tell you which publishers do instant books.)

- What is your book's competition and have you demonstrated that you know how your book *differs* from the competition? Is your book superior? "If you haven't identified any competition," declares editor Carol Meyer, "it's grounds for worry."

This may seem like a forbidding list of questions, but luckily, books are one area in which "there is nothing new under the sun" doesn't seem to apply. "We are blessed with a very large country," says publisher Peter Workman, "and there are tons of books to be done with interest to large blocks of people."

New themes, new topics, new ways of looking at old problems, new ways of using language — the discovery of writers' originality in all its forms is an editor's delight.

THE WONDERFUL WORLD OF *BOOKS IN PRINT*

In nonfiction, *Books in Print* will tell you what's been published on your topic. The massive hardcover tomes of the annually revised *BIP*, organized by title, author, and—most important—subject, can be found in any library. (An annual edition of the *Small Press Record of Books in Print*, edited by Len Fulton and organized by the same categories, is published by Dustbooks.)

Most publishers have *Books in Print* in the office, and the first thing an editor interested in your nonfiction proposal does is check the competition in that year's *BIP*. If the writer has done the necessary homework, Ed should come away from *BIP* feeling even more excited.

Editors scrutinize a nonfiction proposal for its originality because they can't afford to launch a book into the marketplace only to have it crash head-on into stronger competition.

Nonfiction, says editor Jim Landis, is about "tools—sheer information which just happens to be bound in paper. You're not dealing with an aesthetic, so much as with a product. That means marketing must be assessed more carefully." The competition affects decisions, and writers as well as editors need "a comprehensive sense of what is out there at any given time."

Decisions about fiction books are more instinctive. Ed, being well-read, twitches at cliched language, trite themes, hackneyed situations, stories for which the market was exhausted long ago. Any reliance on stereotypes—in notions, characters, plot devices—tends to blind Ed to whatever may be new.

Old plots, however, can always be given new life by a writer with imagination. John Gardner can retell *Beowulf* from the monster's point of view and gets the novel *Grendel*. Ray Bradbury finds the inspirational germ for *The Martian Chronicles* in the plot of Sherwood Anderson's *Winesburg, Ohio*. William Golding gives a new twist to an old book (*The Swiss Family Robinson*) and gets *Lord of the Flies*. And Ed sees a dozen talking animal stories a day—what new things do you have them saying?

A perceptively titled *Writer's Digest* article by writer Sharon Elswit ("Children's Story Plots that Put Editors to Sleep") lists the plots that children's book editors see at least four times a day (the scrawny Christmas tree chosen at the last minute; the elderly neighbor who turns out to love young children; the butterfly that wishes it were a frog) and concludes: "Nobody's saying that you shouldn't write about these topics, but remember that your treatment must be different, stronger, special, and specially written from the child within you."

At any given time, there exist situations and plots that have been done to death. In order to know what these are, writers need to get out and about and away from their desks to investigate their competition.

Being widely read also has the advantage of giving you credibility when you're making a claim as to your own work's originality. A writer might submit a children's book on death and dying, claiming that it's the first book on the subject, unaware that whole bibliographies of similar books exist. Naivete about competition can blind Ed to a book's virtues.

HOW NOT TO COMPETE WITH YOUR OWN PUBLISHER

Ed is *most* conscious of what's already on the publisher's list or forthcoming. To compete with a book that Ed's already published is the kiss of death.

The savvy writer studies the publishing company's output—via catalogs, bookstores, *Publishers Weekly*, and the listings in *BIP*.

Competition with a forthcoming book from your target publisher can be tricky to spot, but it's not impossible. The hefty Fall and Spring Announcements issues of *Publishers Weekly* advertise and describe publishers' adult lists for the upcoming six months. Separate issues display Fall and Spring children's books for the upcoming *year*. The American Booksellers Association (ABA) issue every mid-May is bursting with publishers' (including university presses' and small presses') offerings for the coming autumn. Look through recent back issues for special features on upcoming or recent religious books, mysteries, biographies, small press books, etc.

Still trickier to ascertain is whether or not your book competes with books coming out from other publishers. Nevertheless, this is something Ed is always conscious of—editors usually have a knack for sensing what their rivals are up to. A writer takes a risk in this area. I once accepted a book knowing full well that at least three other publishers were doing similar books, but I was convinced "my" book would be far superior. One top editor tells of evaluating a proposal for a book on the Beach Boys, aware that four other proposals on the same topic were at that moment circulating around town, which affected his decision negatively.

Too-close-for-comfort competition between publishers occasionally occurs—the four simultaneous editions of *The Velveteen Rabbit*, the four concurrent books on the Florida Benson murders. Rarely happening on purpose, it means that a few editors fell asleep at the wheel, or believed their book hugely superior, or saw the market as being large enough to make it worthwhile publishing the books anyway. Editors try to "choose an idea wisely, number one," says publisher Peter Workman, "and then publish it in a way that hasn't been tried before, somehow different or additive."

Here you'll want to research other publishers besides your chosen one, via the methods above. You can also check the Subject Guide to *Forthcoming Books*, a bimonthly supplement to *Books in Print*, carried by most bookstores and libraries. You'll find information about the same books as announced in *PW*, but it will be easier to locate the subjects appropriate to your book.

Also, keep your eyes and ears open for relevant information from writer friends, conferences, newsletters—and your own experience.

If, for instance, you receive a rejection from one publisher saying it's publishing a book nearly identical to yours (something publishers have no reason to lie about), you *may* (especially if it's nonfiction) want to rethink yours before sending it out again: Publisher #2 is very likely to know about Publisher #1's book, and if so, won't want to compete with it unless yours has got a substantial twist.

BEING TOO ORIGINAL

Your book may, in Ed's judgment, be original and fresh, and yet may still present a big problem: Sometimes there's a good *reason* why a book like yours has never been done.

Editors are always looking for the new and the unusual, but sometimes a book will simply strike an editor as too eccentric to publish. Or, to look at it from the writer's point of view, the world may not be ready for your book yet. You may have taken care to write a book to fill a particular gap in the market, but Ed may not see it as a gap that needs filling.

Different editors may have varying attitudes toward a genuinely offbeat vision, and being persistent about sending it out may work. But with publishing as speculative as it is already, most editors feel that original-for-originality's-sake books still have to have a reason for being, i.e., something to say.

If you're lucky enough to hit on an idea with no apparent competition, by all means mention this in your cover letter—but try to head off Ed's nervousness by explaining what noteworthy gap your book fills and why you believe there's a need for it. (If you've really got something revolutionary, you might want to research your publishers for receptiveness to books ahead of their time.)

HOW TO GET TO THE "YES" ANSWER

For this question, almost more than any other, being widely read comes to your rescue.

To begin with, you can get fresh ideas by plugging into the same information networks that inform Ed's vision of the world:

- keeping up with current events via newspapers, a wide range of magazines (from *People* to *The New Yorker*, literary magazines, or whatever are of most interest to you), radio, TV
- reading current books, especially in your field, especially what's selling
- seeing current movies and plays
- reading the trade magazines such as *Publishers Weekly* and *Library Journal*, or *School Library Journal* and *Horn Book* for children's books

- getting out and about, meeting new and interesting people, getting inspiration from family and friends
- researching bookstores regularly
- joining professional organizations and attending writers' conferences, conventions of professionals, and special interest groups
- brainstorming with colleagues
- studying book review sections such as *The New York Times Book Review* (reviews of one book will often stimulate ideas for another)
- researching the market and looking for gaps
- thinking up new twists on public domain material, e.g., classic folktales for children, pamphlets available from the Government Printing Office
- having feelers out in all directions; anticipating trends — being innovative as opposed to trendy
- cultivating a reputation for being receptive to new ideas — which *will* come your way

Unlike Ed, the writer must leave time to *write* amidst all this networking, but a book proposal that derives from one or more of these sources, if it's good, speaks for itself.

In other words, it normally isn't necessary to include in your cover letter the lengths to which you went to get your idea — the magazines you read, the conversations you had. Editors will assume that you're plugged into the same stimulating networks they are.

Savvy writers don't commit a lot of time and energy to a project until they know it's original, and this knowledge can get communicated to Ed by summarizing your *Books in Print* and bookstore research.

MORE ON *BOOKS IN PRINT*

BIP does not list all books in your area of interest, just the new and old ones *in print* that can easily be ordered — including hardcovers, paperbacks, trade books, textbooks, adult and juvenile, technical, and scientific. Check under your subject and any related headings you're directed to or can think of.

The headings, incidentally, correspond to the Library of Congress cataloging information included on a book's copyright page. Fiction books that contain enough factual basis to get them cataloged under the various headings are thus listed in *BIP* as well. (See "World War, 1939-1945," for example.)

Many major headings contain a formidable list of titles — but you'll see that you can rule out textbooks, dated titles, scholarly and academic books, children's books (assuming you're not writing one), or books with a focus obviously alien to yours.

If there is a lot of competition in your area — see "Wines and Wine Making" or "Writing" or "Authors," for example — this isn't *necessarily* a disaster. A perennially popular topic indicates a large market that can often tolerate more books — *if* they have some new angle or are demonstrably superior.

You'll want to check *BIP* eventually because you'll want to start doing the actual research for your book. But investigating the competition now has numerous advantages:

- helping you target your focus and know your audience
- giving you ideas to strengthen your book and set it apart
- telling you immediately if Ed has published a similar book already
- directing you to another publisher without wasting your time and Ed's
- most important: showing Ed that you know what you're doing
- giving you ideas for your *next* book!

Besides checking *BIP* and your in-print competition, also check libraries and bookstores (especially second-hand bookstores) for books *out* of print. Can you come up with reasons *why* the books may have gone out of print?

It also helps to talk to the experts in your specialty — teachers, librarians, booksellers, fans — to get an idea of how they evaluate the competition and any suggestions they have to lend your book more originality.

In your cover letter, list your competition: not every book, just the ones that *seem* to replicate your own idea. Then indicate briefly how your book is superior or different. Condense your evidence so that it's persuasive, not overwhelming.

If you can obtain sales figures for books on your topic (from *Publishers Weekly*, newspaper articles, tips from friends), so much the better: You can mention them to support the popularity of your topic.

DOING THE UNEXPECTED

Once a writer gets into the swing of the kind of research described here, it gets easier and easier to do the unexpected: to take a typical theme and do something so wild that Ed gasps in admiration.

Editors are up to their eyeballs in earnest, plodding manuscripts of the type it seems most beginning writers attempt. With a little homework, it's not that hard to stand out. Editors will love you — or at least sit up and take notice.

A simple tip is to keep all your facts and information thoroughly up-to-date. If you get your proposal back from one editor, read it over before sending it out again to make sure it's still accurate.

Getting rid of your verbal padding will also help — weeding out cliched language, characters, situations.

The most *basic* advice here: Always send out a pristine copy of your work. A dog-eared, yellowing manuscript is the telltale sign of a proposal that's been around a long time. Call them superficial, but editors are known to reject a book on the basis of an aging appearance. They're looking for the new and the different, not the idea that's been rejected by every other publisher in town.

A fresh-looking manuscript will not *guarantee* a "yes" answer to this question, but that plus evidence of homework on your competition will make a big difference.

6.

DOES THE BOOK HAVE INTEGRITY?

Publication—is the auction of the
Mind of Man.
                    —Emily Dickinson

As much outrage as there is about the "gentlemen's profession" plummeting toward conglomerate depths of declining standards and sleazy bestsellers, book publishing still seems to have more integrity than most businesses.

Everyone connected with books—from writer to proofreader to paper supplier to buyer—knows that there is something noble about putting words down on paper and into print. The workings of the human mind *are* somehow sacred, and this reflects on their "auction"—publishing. People in book publishing have high ideals and look for the same in new writers.

Editors tend to be especially caring people, whose love of books enables them to "parent" newly hatched books throughout the entire publishing process. Editors take their work seriously to the point of being what some would call compulsive. They can't afford, in terms of time, money, or energy, to publish writers who consistently let them down in any one of various ways.

Therefore, Ed is very careful, in the early stages of a book's submission, to be alert to its integrity—actually, *your* integrity.

Part of a writer's job, especially if you're unknown to Ed, is to gain Ed's trust in you. Editors are *not* adversaries—really—they simply need writers who can be trusted to carry their own weight.

Ed heeds the same signals *you* might look for when making a friend or hiring an employee. Someone full of stereotypes might offend you, or someone with the bad taste to make ethnic, racial, religious, or sexist slurs. (In particular, the assumption that Ed is a man rubs most Eds—the majority of whom are women—the wrong way.) Traces of narrow-mindedness or condescension will bother an editor, as will bragging, especially of the "this-book-will-make-millions-for-you" type.

In a friend, you'd look for evidence of sincerity and truthfulness, and any type of lie—an inconsistency between actions and words or even a significant omission of the truth—will turn an editor off. Yes, promote yourself, but not to the point of including outright lies likely to be spotted.

People who make promises they can't or don't keep might make you nervous. Ed, too. For instance, the ability to meet deadlines is one hallmark of a professional. If, in the early stages of a proposal, you promise to send additional information by a certain date and don't, or don't respond promptly to requests for revision, or promise something physically impossible, Ed starts losing confidence.

THE SECOND BEST-KEPT SECRET IN EDITORS' OFFICES

If you include inaccurate or inconsistent information, it will seem to editors as though you are trying to pull something over on them.

The same is true of grammatical carelessness. "The second best-kept secret in editors' offices," claims a recent *Writer's Digest* ad, is that a "major reason manuscripts are rejected is poor grammar." Ed will seldom go to the trouble of telling you that grammatical errors were the reason for rejection, but this is because Ed hasn't read much further into the material to determine what larger flaws (or virtues) it may have.

One mistake won't kill a book, but a slew of them sends a mixed message: On the one hand, you want to get published. On the other hand, perhaps you don't take what you're doing seriously enough to construct a sentence correctly or double-check your spelling. Ed usually doesn't have time to sort out the truth.

Equally nerve-wracking are typos, which can reflect as much on a new writer's integrity as powerful writing or *au courant* research. Again, one typo won't make Ed throw the book out the window, but a number of them demonstrate a careless attitude that Ed cannot afford to encourage.

Everyone makes typos — that's why the people who invented spell-checkers in word-processing programs are so wealthy — but writers working on gaining Ed's trust won't risk sending out un-proofread work. Typos tell Ed (rightly or wrongly) that the writer's not the sort who can be trusted.

Great writers take great care with their writing. Gustave Flaubert once spent a whole weekend pondering one punctuation mark: On Saturday he changed a comma from Friday's work to a semicolon, on Sunday he changed it back to a comma, and this to him was a good weekend's work.

Editors work hard. Some writers work even harder, of course, but an unfortunate percentage are what Ed would term "lazy." Writing *is* work, and evidence that the writer thinks otherwise makes your editor cranky.

There's nothing wrong with wanting to make money from writing, but sometimes writers transparently display this as their sole motive. This lack of integrity troubles Ed, who will foresee difficulties ahead in working toward a finished book.

Ed is always looking for signs that a book is well thought out:

• Are your facts error-free and consistent, your quotations accurate? Book publishers, unlike many magazines, do not employ fact-checkers and will reject a book that seems to assume this sort of homework.

• Is your research up-to-date? Can it be independently verified — are your steps logical enough for Ed or a freelance expert to trace?

• Does the proposal contain everything Ed needs to make a decision, or do you send along afterthoughts (very aggravating)?

• Have you been persistent with your research, tracking down that last fact or reference to solidify your proposal?

- Are you serious about your work, or are you an opportunist hoping to capitalize on the latest fad?

- Do you submit your rough drafts, assuming Ed will somehow see the hidden potential in them?

- Have you thought through all aspects of your material? Have you distanced yourself from it or gotten others, even an expert consultant, to read and comment on it?

- Have you considered alternative treatments, methods, choices, and concluded that yours are still the best?

- Is your belief in yourself based on some solid evidence?

ARE YOU THE "REAL THING?"

Very frequently, a writer will get a rejection letter saying that something is "too slight for a book." Translation: A writer gets a good idea and then lets it go at that, without thinking it through past the first draft. Or it might have been a great idea but for a magazine article, without the substantial development a book requires. It's frustrating for an editor to watch good ideas get as far as getting written down on paper—and then get dropped like hot potatoes.

Editors look for writers who took their time to think, who let an idea germinate and flower before rushing it off, still warm from their printers, to an editor.

Editors, much as they might even like to, cannot do this kind of thinking for a writer. Besides not having time, they're not necessarily competent to do it: If editors could write your books, they'd be on the other side of the desk.

On the other hand, if you *have* done your thinking and are justifiably proud of your work, do you defend it? Or will you compromise yourself at the least urging? In Doris Lessing's *The Golden Notebook*, the writer-heroine meets with her editor and agrees unquestioningly to a major change. The editor, however, "had hoped I would not compromise; although it is her job to see that I should. . . . Her manner changes subtly: She is handling a writer who is prepared to sacrifice integrity to get a story on to television."

It's a delicate balance writers tread, between being thought a pain in the posterior and being thought a wimp. No one can tell a writer exactly where to draw the line, but developing one's personal integrity will help.

WHY LAWYERS ARE WEALTHY

One telling sign of a responsible writer is awareness of the legal side of writing. Legal troubleshooting is part of Ed's job:

• Have you plagiarized anyone else's ideas or material?

• Have you borrowed song lyrics or extensive text quotations without indicating the need to obtain permission from the copyright owners?

• Do you libel or defame anyone—do you say nasty and/or untrue things about a real person, alive or dead, or about a character based on an identifiable real person?

• Do you invade anyone's privacy, disclosing distorted or embarrassing information—or just plain information the person doesn't want disclosed?

• If you're writing fiction, do you use real names of people who are likely to become upset and even threaten a lawsuit?

• Are you up-front with Ed about what's real in your work and what you've made up?

• Do you wreak havoc with known facts, creating troublesome inaccuracies?

• Do you substantiate assertions, especially controversial ones? Do you corroborate your information with reliable sources?

• Do you keep records of interviews and research in case any of your facts are questioned later?

• Have you included directions that could cause harm—

potentially dangerous cooking instructions in a book for children, for example? Does the book contain any information that could endanger anyone's life — national secrets, for example?

These and many other questions make lawyers wealthy.

Naivete regarding legal matters is by no means limited to new writers. I once accepted a novel from an author of some forty books, who — I was dismayed to learn — had used the names of real people for his latest characters and had unquestionably defamed them. Fancy footwork with the legal department was required to disguise these characters beyond recognition.

In another case, a popular author used real names for subjects interviewed on an extremely personal topic (and had not gotten them to sign release forms giving him permission to use the information in a book) — any of whom would have been happy to sue later, had we not taken care to disguise their identities and get them to sign releases.

Another time, an artist sprinkled throughout his illustrations characters created by other artists and also licensed, copyrighted cartoon figures — characters for which license fees must be paid and permission gotten before they can be used. If you look at his book carefully, you'll see places where more generic characters have been inserted as replacements.

After signing up a book, Ed works closely with the in-house legal department to resolve problems in manuscript stage. Lawsuits can zap a book's profits and other books' as well, not to mention the publisher's credibility and the editor's job. The laws regarding writing are not always clear-cut, and some court cases even seem to contradict one another. But once your book is accepted, you can rely on the publisher's expertise, which in almost all cases will make the book lawsuit-proof.

In the meantime, Ed is not inclined to sign up books that seem to invite legal trouble. And you should be aware that most publishing contracts, under the warranty and indemnity clause, make the writer responsible for claims or lawsuits arising from a book's publication. Publishers do go to court to defend their books, but have also been known to sue *writers* who deliberately deluded them.

It's highly recommended that writers consult legal guides,

such as *How to Bulletproof Your Manuscript* by Bruce Henderson (who reports that plaintiffs *win* in 83 percent of libel cases), or the "legal issues" chapters in writers' guidebooks. If you have major questions, consult a lawyer before sending your work out.

All editors are paranoid about legal disasters, and like James Silberman, look for "authors who are reliable, who have self-respect, and who do their homework."

Ed looks for evidence that you take yourself, the law, the English language, your subject, your audience, and your publisher seriously. Whew! This may *seem* like a tall order, but a writer with integrity automatically has the "right stuff."

HOW TO GET TO THE "YES" ANSWER

In all aspects of your presentation—from your attitude to your facts to your "thanks for considering my work"—it's to your advantage to cultivate an atmosphere of mutual respect. You have no history or particular clout with Ed at the moment. You may have talent and integrity to spare, but unless you make the traditional, expected moves, Ed can get scared off.

Some unprofessional writers *are* genuine trouble (to the point where several major publishers will no longer even open unsolicited manuscripts), and experienced editors are inclined to operate under the Napoleonic code—wherein a new writer is "trouble" until proven otherwise. You have the right to be treated respectfully and in a businesslike way, and no more.

Editors aren't merely being crabby when they react negatively to signs of amateurism—these are also warnings that you won't be an author Ed's company can be proud of. Whether or not you've had practice representing a company before, you and your book, once published, will be forever associated with that publisher.

Says one bookseller: "Nothing sticks in the mind of the bookseller or the reviewer longer than the self-aggrandizing promoter who tells untruths about The New Book regardless of reality. Honesty counts. Integrity is vital."

Ed looks for people who show class and integrity *now* — who aren't tacky or deceitful — because Ed can foresee *the future*.

ATTENTION TO DETAIL

Before sending something out, pay close attention to directory listings, or the guidelines publishers may send you on request. It's arrogant to assume that you can change company policy or dispense with the publisher's various requirements. Also, it's a waste of your time to send unsolicited manuscripts when publishers specifically say they won't look at them, or send a manuscript when they ask to see queries only, or — especially — send submissions inappropriate to the house. Don't make phone calls, or try to substitute talking about your work for letting Ed *read* it.

None of this is meant to insult you. But part of what Ed looks for is attention to detail and the ability to listen and observe — and ignoring publishers' requirements is a usually fatal case of getting off on the wrong foot. First impressions count. Ignoring the basics of manuscript preparation (Question #1) shows a lack of integrity. So does sending out historical fiction that contains anachronisms, or any writing that's flawed by the inconsistencies mentioned earlier. Referring to his reputation for scrupulous research, bestselling author Tom Clancy says, "I feel a moral obligation to my readers to get it right."

It's not a good idea to leave in mistakes for the copyeditors to catch, or to use TV as a model for grammar. When *Dynasty*'s Blake Carrington shouts at Alexis, "How could you do that — when I *implicitly* told you . . ." and he means "*ex*plicitly," change the station, or better yet, pick up a book.

(And *do* you support the book community? "I've had it with these cheap sons of bitches who claim they love poetry but never buy a book," says poet Kenneth Rexroth. Ed similarly rails against writers who write but clearly don't read, or who want to get published but won't increase other writers' sales figures. I've looked at untold numbers of children's book attempts by writers who hadn't bought a children's book since their childhood — and it *shows*. Are you doing anything to fight illiteracy — by either working with illiterates, or writing books that *compel*? What are you, as a responsible writer, doing to ensure that this generation of readers won't be the last?)

THE BOOK SPEAKS FOR ITSELF

In your cover letter, it works against you to exaggerate credits or accomplishments to the point of lying. When Rahila Khan, the talk of London's literary world as a young Islamic girl, was revealed in 1987 to be the pen name of a middle-aged Anglican priest, his publisher was so furious it dropped him from the list and announced plans to withdraw his books from bookstores. "To be known as a liar in the book trade is suicidal," says a top American editor.

Don't be chummy or cute with an editor you don't know. And book editors don't steal ideas; it's the sign of the amateur to worry about it.

Let your work speak for itself. Don't include testimonials from friends or relatives. "My grandchildren loved this and want to hear it again and again," a writer will say. Children love it when their parents or grandparents read to them enthusiastically—the choice of story is secondary. Testimonials from unknowns, as much as they might rightfully mean to you, carry no weight with Ed and will be interpreted as a presumptuous underestimation of Ed's editorial judgment. Quoting rival editors has the same effect.

Never apologize for your work (why give Ed an out?), but if you want to lend support, mention the statistics, sales figures, and results of surveys you gathered while researching Question #4.

Rather than using Ed as your writing teacher or first reader, sit on your material before sending it out. You're guaranteed to find simple mistakes, room for improvements, and—eureka!—more ideas. There's really no point in rushing a half-baked proposal to Ed: The good half will get rejected right along with the underdone half.

Writer Raymond Carver recommended a "real seriousness in what you're doing. You want it right and you don't have that many chances at it. I don't know how many books a person's going to take to the grave with him, but you want to have it right, or else what's the point?"

Ed would be the first to agree.

HOW TO ACT AROUND EDITORS

It helps to be realistic about the manuscript review process, without harassing Ed about making a decision too quickly. After two months with no word, write a letter (don't phone). Asking if your material "arrived safely" is a tactful way of nudging Ed. Another month, and then it's acceptable to phone, or to write again—writers must use their own judgment. Editors truly are sympathetic about how long writers wait for decisions, but they also have direct experience with the crushing amount of work on their desks already.

Any sense that you are bending the traditional manuscript submission guidelines in order to "put something over" on an editor will offend that editor—very likely to the point of rejecting your book. For example, one rule in multiple submissions is that you're always upfront with your target editor that your book *is* a multiple submission. Theoretically, you could decide to keep this information to yourself, in which case one editor's acceptance will put you in the position of having to call the other editors and withdraw your book from consideration. Most editors will feel like fools for wasting energy on a project that others were looking at and are unlikely to want to see more from you in the future.

If Ed wants to meet with you to discuss your work, it is definitely to your advantage to comport yourself with dignity, and treat Ed with courtesy. I've sat through meals with authors who complained that if they didn't get higher advances they'd have to go to *work* for a living—which can raise an underpaid working person's hackles.

When one writer who'd sent in a manuscript showed up for a lunch appointment with several family members in tow, I decided on a sandwich place to save the company a small fortune—whereupon she kept disappearing to the bar around the corner, leaving me to chat awkwardly with her family. Her behavior deteriorated, until eventually I knew no matter what wonderful books she was writing, I didn't want to publish them. She had, unfortunately for me, published some fine books with other companies, so it was not an easy decision to make.

But the experience taught me something, as did lots of *positive* experiences with authors who later became good friends: Editors are human beings and don't have to publish writers who denigrate that status.

There's a whole book called *Professional Etiquette for Writers*, by William Brohaugh, that helps a writer momentarily walk in an editor's shoes, and which demonstrates that editorial etiquette is not a boggling foreign language, but—like much else in publishing—mostly a matter of common sense.

Editorial good manners are but one sign of an integrity that illuminates a writer's work. Another sign, besides those mentioned already, is a belief in yourself strong enough to withstand the discouragement of a few rejections.

Demonstrating integrity will always increase a book's chances for acceptance and, eventually, your success in the auction of the Mind of Man.

7.

HOW MUCH EDITORIAL WORK WILL THE BOOK REQUIRE?

No passion in the world is equal to the passion to alter someone else's draft.
—H.G. Wells

For better or for worse, editorial alterations are usually not what Ed wants to be thinking about at this stage. Rather, the key sentiment for the typical editor is: "How much of my time is this book going to need?"

Improving on a manuscript is a traditional function of the editor—the editor as Shaper, occasionally the editor as Surgeon. "A reader sees a printed book and that's it," says writer E.L. Doctorow, but an editor is "at ease in the book the way a surgeon is at ease in a human chest, with all the blood and guts and everything."

Ed generally has a knack for asking the questions that will draw the best material out of you, which is, of course, part of Ed's job. "Two qualities that distinguish the professional editor," writes A. Scott Berg about Maxwell Perkins, are "the vision to see beyond the faults of a good book, no matter how dismaying; and the tenacity to keep working, through all discouragements, toward the book's potential."

But at book-evaluation time, overworked editors fret about the amount of work required to reach that potential. Some editors get known for making good books better; some can even make bad books good. But no editors ever knowingly let themselves in for rewriting or becoming an anonymous co-author. No child was ever heard to say, "I want to be a manuscript doctor when I grow up."

As with reading manuscripts, editing them is a task Ed often performs after hours. Whether it's light editing, suggesting changes, heavy editing, or a major overhaul, there is no time during a typical office day for the concentrated, intense labor of picking apart a book from every conceivable angle.

Ed usually can't invest equal time in each book. Sometimes there are "problem" books that absorb 80 percent of Ed's time, leaving the other 20 percent to be divided among the rest as best as possible. Even "normal" books with "normal" amounts of editorial work take up time, generating queries on everything from structural and stylistic intricacies to problems with the content to internal difficulties that, as editor Thomas McCormack puts it, "may have no obvious fixed address in the manuscript." Editor Jim Landis once edited a manuscript on which he had six queries per page—only it was a 1,200-page manuscript, so that meant more than 7,000 flagged queries—and this was but one of the thirty-six books he was editing that year.

Such being the real world of an editor, Ed gravitates toward grown-up writers. "It is the job of the author to write a masterpiece," intones editor Cyril Connolly. But it's not a perfect world, and unless you're Henry Miller (who wouldn't allow a word of his writing to be edited), your project will require at least some editorial time.

Editors, not to be confused with writing teachers, appreciate evidence that you know what you're doing. "Great editing is not possible without great books to edit," says one well-known editor. Editors especially resent the assumption that they exist to clean up your writing. The ultimate responsibility (as well as the credit) for the book's quality is the author's.

In looking at your manuscript or query, Ed tries to decide whether it's an editorially labor-intensive project or a relatively labor-free one:

- Is your book complete, or do you have years left to go on it?

- Does what you've done need a lot of revision? What exactly are the weaknesses, and are they major (structural) or minor (easily fixed)?

• How much writing experience do you have? Are you the right person to complete the necessary revisions, or to do the book at all?

• Is there a spark of a good book here? There are those manuscripts, says one editor, that "even Oral Roberts couldn't raise . . . from the dead."

• Do you have more books in you? "Will working on this book and giving it an enormous amount of time and encouragement," asks editor Page Cuddy, "make it possible for [you] to write a second book that will not require this kind of attention?"

• If it's a query or proposal, have you done similar work that demonstrates you're capable of delivering what you promise? Are you already clearly on the right track? Can Ed follow the steps of your thinking?

• Is your attitude pleasant? Are you easy to work with, professional, dedicated, or do you make unreasonable claims and demands? Are you serious about your work and willing to be guided toward making it better?

No need to panic at questions like these! Depending on the strength of their answers to Question #1, editors *do* accept books that require substantial revision or with much work left to go. If the book is complete *and* good, so much the better, but one reason Ed makes most decisions on the basis of queries and sample chapters is the chance this gives for early shaping — avoiding the possibility of major revisions later.

Ed does this in an atmosphere of mutual trust and is extremely careful about deciding which books to take on.

EDITORS EDITING

An editor and writer "must have a shared vision of what should be done in the manuscript's best interests," says consultant

Nancy Evans. Just getting the proposal in front of Ed's editorial board can demand much editorial back-and-forth. If this doesn't go smoothly or Ed has to do work you oppose, it makes for an unsatisfactory relationship that wastes Ed's energy. Ed can still say "no."

Ed, the proverbial "fresh eye," appreciates writers who accept editing when necessary. According to one editor, most writers are frantic to know: "What is it like to read this book? Does the writing work as an exciting reading experience? Where are my loose ends?" A high point of most editors' jobs is being able to answer these questions for writers they trust.

Writers who have worked both sides of the desk treasure a good editor's vision. As an editor herself, Pulitzer prize-winning writer Toni Morrison says that "piercing knots in language and in ideas, assisting in the discovery of clarity, connections, illustrations, tone are what editing requires." And as a writer, she "always takes the editor's comments seriously, because even if they are not on target, the fact that the editor is restless about something is important."

E.L. Doctorow, a former editor, claims editing "taught me how to break books down and put them back together. You learn . . . the value of . . . keeping tension on the page and how that's done, and you learn how to spot self-indulgence. . . . You learn how to become very free and easy about moving things around." Laurie Colwin, another ex-editor, says, "There is nothing that can't be made better."

Some writers rate their writing careers by the editing they've received. Notice how many books are dedicated to editors. John Irving, in enumerating editors he's worked with, concludes, "I've been *very* lucky, and I know it, and I'm grateful." John Hersey mourns, "I don't think I had as much editing as I would have liked to have on my books."

Most writers know that a good editor is worth his or her weight in gold:

- "He demanded more of me than I had and thereby caused me to be more than I should have been without him," wrote John Steinbeck in dedicating *East of Eden* to his editor (who supplied everything from guidance to a steady quota of pencils and yellow legal pads).

- Editing *Final Payments*, Mary Gordon's editor pointed out a discrepancy that resulted in Gordon's writing one of the most critically acclaimed scenes in the book.

- When none of Peter Benchley's nonfiction ideas were working out, his editor suggested a novel, the result being *Jaws*.

- Maurice Sendak's editor asked questions . . . and she *kept* asking them until he devised the "inevitable" ending to *Where the Wild Things Are*.

- In common with many authors, Julius Lester had written only adult books when an editor suggested he try a children's book; the result in his case was *To Be a Slave*, a Newbery Honor Book.

- Editing *The Arrangement*, Elia Kazan's editor drew a picture of "external female genitalia" and said his heroine had no other characteristics thus far; Kazan's subsequent changes were the "critical point in the editing process" of a huge bestseller.

The best writers shoulder "editorial work" themselves — by editing their own work. "A writer's best work comes entirely from himself," according to Maxwell Perkins, who always downplayed his legendary work with his legendary authors. (For the most in-depth look at how editors actually deal with manuscripts, see A. Scott Berg's *Max Perkins: Editor of Genius*. For a rare movie portrayal of an editor at work, see *Cross Creek*, which has Perkins working with Marjorie Kinnan Rawlings, author of *The Yearling*.)

Revising can be painful:

- William Faulkner saw it as murdering "all my little darlings."

- "I have rewritten — often several times — every word I have ever published," said Vladimir Nabokov. "My pencils outlast their erasers."

- Bernard Malamud writes every story and novel three

times: "Once to understand it, the second time to improve the prose, and a third to compel it to say what it still must say."

- Raymond Carver admitted to "as many as twenty to thirty drafts of a story. Never less than ten or twelve drafts."

- Tolstoy rewrote *War and Peace* eight times and was still tinkering with it in galleys.

- Nora Ephron goes everyone a step further and uses 300 to 400 sheets of paper to get one six-page essay.

- Or perhaps Philip Roth is the winner, with six months of eight-hour days to produce one good page.

Writers dedicated to the art of revision, something a writer is best qualified to do, are what Ed looks for. "It is the editor's ultimate task to make himself dispensable," as one top editor puts it.

Other things being equal, Ed will almost always choose a book needing little editing over a book needing a lot.

HOW TO GET TO THE "YES" ANSWER

The obvious answer here is to write the best book you can—easy to say!

It helps to start by making your manuscript or proposal as complete as is possible to sell it. Publishers vary on what they want to see. Whole books exist on this topic (see Bibliography). Check the listings in *Writer's Market* or *Novel & Short Story Writer's Market* before sending anything. Or write for the guidelines many publishers send out upon request. Or make a brief call to the editorial department and *ask* what its policy is. It's not necessary to give your name or start up a discussion—just ask the secretary or editorial assistant you reach what the publisher wants to see for the type of material you're writing.

As always, neatness, good proofreading, and skill with grammar will all signal how much of the nitty-gritty work you're leaving up to the editor—preferably not much.

It's unrealistic to assume that Ed is going to be your co-writer. "An editor's job is to shape the *expression* of an author's thoughts, not the thoughts themselves," stresses Arthur Plotnik in *The Elements of Editing*. Not submitting your first draft will demonstrate your realistic attitude: the difference between a professional and an amateur.

When I give talks to schoolchildren, I bring along the drafts for a piece of writing, showing flabbergasted children how sometimes five or six drafts are necessary before what you want to say emerges clearly. When Nora Ephron was in college, she *never* revised: "I wrote out my papers in longhand, typed them up and turned them in. It would never have crossed my mind that what I had produced was only a first draft and that I had more work to do; the idea was to get to the end, and once you had got to the end you were finished."

Professional writers operate differently. They *think like an editor*, scrutinizing their work from a not-necessarily-sympathetic point of view.

Loose ends will make Ed cringe, so it's to your advantage to check the logic of your thoughts for possible holes in your plot or chapters out of sequence. Being in a terrific hurry to get from a great Point A to a great Point B can create great drivel in between.

If you find questions coming up as you read over your material, try to answer them somehow. Ed will not be calling you up to ask, "What did you mean by this sentence here?" or "How do you get Point B out of Point A?" or "Just how do you propose to accomplish what you promise?"

Instead, Ed moves on to the next package, perhaps with a twinge of regret at having to pass by the germ of a good idea that was left undeveloped.

ARE YOU EXPERIENCED?

Ed, in responding to your book, plays the role of Jimi Hendrix, asking "Are You Experienced?" In your cover letter, stress the professional writing experience you've had, and minimize any gaps. In a query letter, it's a good idea to indicate that you realize what work is left to do, and that you're willing and able to do it. Emphasize your ability and your desire to complete the book.

If your writing credits are slim, don't bluff or resort to half-truths, but don't apologize or express doubts, either. In trying to exude an aura of quiet confidence, it's a great advantage to send out only work that you *are* confident of.

When developing a realistic, healthy attitude toward revision, you'll see that Ed is not an enemy out to destroy you but a person doing a job. "As long as writers write primarily to advance themselves, and editors edit to satisfy readers, there will never be a lasting peace," writes Arthur Plotnik.

Still, the attitude of mutual respect you cultivated for Question #6 will stand you in good stead here as well. "You write to communicate to the hearts and minds of others what's burning inside you," Plotnik likes to tell writing classes, "and we edit to let the fire show through the smoke." Both sides deserve respect.

Mutual respect includes respecting yourself. Writers with integrity know instinctively when to stick to their guns when asked to make changes that could compromise the work. Being an active participant in your revisions is much more to your advantage than being a mute spectator.

ON NOT BEING A GLUTTON FOR PUNISHMENT

In your initial cover letter, don't *ask* for suggestions for revision—it's the sign of an amateur. If editors are interested in your work, they'll make suggestions on their own. Always keep an exact duplicate of whatever you've sent to editors, in case they call you to discuss it over the phone or hold on to your material.

If editors aren't interested, they don't wrestle with a writer—it makes the review process more exhausting than it already is. Ed knows from experience that when most writers ask for suggestions, they want to hear, "Cut page 43 and we'll publish your book." As you can see by now, publishing doesn't work like this.

Unless editors are genuinely interested in your work, they seldom spell out reasons for rejection. No matter what reason Ed gives, nine out of ten times writers will resent it, and it's hard to blame them. I think it's insulting to tell a writer why you're rejecting a manuscript. Rejection is painful enough already.

Once you do start a relationship with an editor, take it seriously and don't revise to please other "editors." If Ed's advice is contradicted by your writing teacher's, your mate's, your children's, or your literary-minded Uncle Harold's, it's worth your while to listen to Ed.

You can take as much advice as you want to beforehand (although no less a writer than Robert Heinlein insists that "you must refrain from rewriting except to editorial order"), but once you start getting direction from Ed, tune the others out:

- Your writing teacher isn't going to publish your work, Ed is.
- No one knows the market and the publishing company like Ed does.
- It's physically impossible to incorporate suggestions from all sides; I've worked with writers who nearly drove themselves and me crazy trying.

AN INCESTUOUS SUGGESTION

In order to *get* an editor interested in publishing your book, a writer can learn more about the craft of self-editing. This many sound somehow incestuous, but all it means is doing a little homework before submitting something for publication. Take a course or two in editing, or look at some of the books listed in the Bibliography, particularly *The Elements of Editing, Editors on Editing, The Fiction Editor, Revision, Bookmaking*, and *Words into Type* (which isn't called *WIT* for nothing), to see how editors actually edit.

In-house editing is sweaty, hard work, and often thankless to boot. One of the highest compliments I could pay an author would be to say, "Editing your work is a pleasure." If the editing indeed *was* fun, it meant the authors had done my work for me—or actually their own work for themselves.

Knowing something about editing and revision puts a writer that much further ahead when it comes to concentrating on your *first* priority: writing.

PART 2

MARKETING QUESTIONS

8.

WHAT ARE YOUR CREDENTIALS FOR WRITING THIS BOOK?

The editorial job has become, unlike the ancient age when one judged what one read, a job of making judgments on outlines, ideas, reputations, previous books, scenarios, treatments, talk, and promises.

— Sam Vaughn

To answer the question "Is this a good book?"—it shouldn't be necessary to know what you've done before.

But once editors deal with the preceding seven keys to their own satisfaction, they enlarge their horizons. It's time to generate house enthusiasm and lay the groundwork for getting the right book to the right buyers at the right time. In accomplishing this, Ed doesn't work alone.

The people who actually market and sell the books Ed signs up are usually the first to be consulted. If the marketing people, who make excellent sounding boards, like your proposed book—think they can sell it—editors know they're on to something.

And the marketing people, to sell your book, want to know about certain *extra*-editorial factors: They want a one-sentence handle for *you*. This sentence, like the "handle" for your book in Question #3, will get used in catalog copy, sales presentations, advertising, jacket copy, sub-rights presentations, reviews, introductions by trendy new talk show hosts, and so on.

So editors, particularly if they work for commercial houses, ask important questions now:

• Are you a "name" author—will your book sell partly on the strength of your name alone?

• What other books have you published? What are their sales figures? What kind of reviews did they get? Any special recognition—national or local awards, special mentions, "best of the year" lists, etc.?

• Do you have high visibility in your field? Are you well-connected, with influential contacts willing to supply blurbs (laudatory quotes to appear on your book jacket or in possible advertising)?

• Are you a known quantity among readers, or among publishers—possibly for the wrong reasons? Do you have the reputation of a winner or a loser?

Ed takes your credentials into account partly to satisfy marketing demands, partly out of legitimate editorial need, and partly out of human curiosity.

Editors, you'll remember, are first and foremost only readers. Like a particularly famous reader, they want to know about you and feel that you're approachable: Holden Caulfield, in J. D. Salinger's *The Catcher in the Rye* (which, incidentally, endured twenty rejections before it was published), rates the books he reads by the strength of his feeling that the author is a friend he'd like to call up.

Writer Erica Jong used to love certain authors so much that she'd kiss their pictures on the book jackets. E. L. Doctorow goes further: "In one sense the task of a professional writer who publishes books is to overcome the terrible loss of not being someone the reader knows and loves."

Editors really want to know and like you. According to publisher David Godine, the impulse to publish derives not only from attraction to a subject, but also to an author: "If it's a subject, you try to determine whether this author knows more about it, or can do a better job on that subject, than any other author. . . . If it's an author you're betting on, you're basically betting on the future of the author as a writer and on his qualities as a human being." Godine, for one, would never publish an author he hadn't met.

Many editors would agree, which is why getting published can sometimes seem like such a Catch-22 (the title for Joseph Heller's book, which, incidentally, was conceived by his editor): Editors publish "who they know," but how do you get known until you're published?

It's true—solid credentials and playing "who you know" make life easier, just as they do when you're looking for a new babysitter, hiring a typist, finding a dentist or therapist. It's human nature to want to protect ourselves from unknown potential crazies. Editors, being human also, hesitate to invest money and time in untried authors.

Ed wants to know your credentials for writing *this* book:

• What are your areas of expertise? What qualifies *you* to write on this particular topic? Will outside experts need to be hired to go over your work?

• What writing experience have you had? Have you published related articles in local or national magazines or newspapers?

• Do you show a progression in your writing? Do you have a career that Ed sees as having promise?

• Have you taught or otherwise made a living from what you're writing about? How are you *involved* with it? What special circumstances led to your writing this book?

• Does your experience demonstrate a *passion* for your topic and for writing? To what lengths have you gone to get your material and research?

THE WRITER AS A HUMAN BEING

Ed makes judgments about more human factors as well:

• Are you intelligent and cooperative—a professional? Do

you have the integrity discussed in Question #6?

- Do you show willingness to work and revise?

- Or is it immediately obvious that you're a "difficult" author — unstable, unrealistic, stubborn? Do you assume the position of Ed's adversary?

- Are you prejudiced in some way — do you have a bias or an ax to grind, rather than a point of view?

Ed and the marketing department will try to predict your promotion potential. "The consideration of the author as a public personality is coming to be less and less a matter of pure chance," according to Thomas Whiteside, author of *The Blockbuster Complex*. Editor Kathryn Court agrees: "On certain sorts of books . . . meeting with authors and getting a real sense of how able they are to talk really well about their subject makes a difference."

Writer Pat Conroy electrified booksellers at a convention with a reading from his forthcoming *Prince of Tides*, and then watched his first bestseller take off. Judith Krantz, known to autograph 500 copies of *Scruples* an hour, claims to have "been on every local TV show that has ever existed." Colleen McCullough used to autograph more than 2,000 books *a day*. Bret Easton Ellis sees promotion as part of being a contemporary writer: "The company invests time and money in publishing your book, so there is a part of me that says, 'OK, you do owe them to go out and hustle around and sell some books for them.' "

Not all types of books require this sort of effort, but in general, Ed tries to discern your potential:

- Are you personable — enthusiastic, articulate, excited? Can you convey all this on paper until such time as you meet with Ed?

- Are you willing and able to promote yourself and your book, if it's called for? Will you be an asset to the sales force, or do you feel that marketing and promotion are "beneath" you?

- Will you be a "team player" with the sales staff, or will you be off in a corner playing your own game?

• Are you a "tourable" kind of author—the type who can patiently autograph books for hours, who can make appearances and charm strangers into marching straight to their bookstores, who can answer the same questions over and over without betraying exhaustion or irritation?

THE LURE OF THE UNKNOWN

Once again, all these nosy, persistent questions need not make a writer panic. *Not* having a string of bestsellers behind you by no means stops publishable books from getting published. Ed is always looking for the new and the different—including authors.

Perhaps your talent overrides a lack of credentials. "The discovery of new talent," says publisher Robert Giroux, "is the greatest reward that comes from editorial work." New talent, by definition, isn't heavily credentialed, and the detection of it is the *raison d'être* for most editors.

Editors are attracted as much to talented strangers as to "who they know." They've always been lured by writers of a tender age, or who seem to have sprung full-blown from nowhere. Ed frequently succumbs to the exhilaration of discovery, the speeded-up heartbeat of a good gamble.

Everyone started out unpublished, and optimism springs eternal in Ed's breast that you'll be the next star. "There aren't enough Micheners and Kings and Krantzes to go around for all of the publishers," says agent Albert Zuckerman. "So there's an enormous competition for the new boy [girl] in town."

A writer should never let minimal credentials be discouraging. The fact is: Most editors want to be perceived as responsible for midwifing the birth of the next fair-haired child; thus they can be more receptive to *first* novels than to seconds or thirds. What editor would not want to claim responsibility for

Gone with the Wind
From Here to Eternity
This Side of Paradise
Bright Lights, Big City

The Naked and the Dead
Carrie
The Sun Also Rises
Peyton Place
Valley of the Dolls
Day of the Jackal
Ordinary People
The Cat Ate My Gymsuit
Lord of the Flies
Presumed Innocent
The Clan of the Cave Bear
The Women's Room
Scruples
The Beans of Egypt, Maine

—all of which were first novels? "First novelists are the lifeblood of this business," insists publisher Oscar Dystel.

Lack of credentials, then, is not a disaster, but Ed looks for factors to compensate—talent, a hot topic, a book that comes alive or blazes a trail. Personal charm can help, but will not by itself do the trick. Ed, being a *reader*, seldom buys a book on the basis of the author's animal magnetism alone. The words on the page have to be of equal magnetism.

"You need a book with intrinsic value," says one top editor, "even if it's frivolous intrinsic value." Conversely, says Thomas Whiteside, "It is unlikely that any manuscript would be turned down because the author told his prospective publisher that he had no intention of going on TV or radio to plug the work."

AN EDITOR'S "ONE-SENTENCE HANDLE"

Editors often try to determine at this point whether they're likely to want *more* books from you. The sales force likes having more than one book by the same author—it makes the books easier to sell, and sales for each book tend to be higher. "Publishers naturally spend more money on house authors than on those who have many publishers," says one commercial editor.

An editor's identity, or "one-sentence handle" (in a *Publishers Weekly* article, say, or a job application), *is* the list of authors he or she works with and has built up. When editors get promoted, it's because of "their" authors, not just individual books. As Arthur Plotnik puts it, "Book editors acquire, not just money-making manuscripts, but market-rated authors to haul from house to house."

Editors, when investing time and energy in your first book, want to see the fruits of their labors when you write your second and third. And if the future books are *better* books, which is frequently the case, Ed wants to be around to take part in the joyous experience—and to take credit for getting you started by signing you up in the first place.

An editor is "buying into somebody's whole career," says one literary editor. "If it is likely that you are going to want the next book and beyond it, that definitely increases the value of the book you are particularly negotiating for." A commercial editor agrees: "We're looking for writers who will go on writing, and, ideally, grow and develop, not just for a person who is momentarily with book."

When editors believe you have great books in you, they'll sometimes gamble on a first book they know is not going to be a great book or sell well. Looking toward the future is part of Ed's job. As editor Bill Whitehead points out, there's a "healthy tension" between the marketing department, "who tend to look back, and want to rely upon an author's track record," and the editors, "who go with expectations for the future."

In any case, future reward is how Ed will justify to the editorial board the wisdom of signing up a chancy book—your *next* book will make it worth signing up *this* one!

That's why all publishing contracts contain, unless you negotiate to have it removed, an option clause giving the publisher the right of first refusal on your next book: Publishers feel you "owe" them that for investing in you in the first place. At least one publisher negotiates "a multi-book contract or nothing," feeling that if his house "is to back a book or build an author, it needs the incentive of a guaranteed ongoing relationship." Most editors look for that loyalty, even if it's not in writing.

This doesn't mean that you, in trying to sell your book to

Ed now, need to promise away your lifetime's work. But signs that you have more books in you are guaranteed to increase Ed's interest.

HOW TO GET TO THE "YES" ANSWER

In your cover letter, your job is to inspire Ed's confidence — or at least, to convince Ed that you're not crazy, but rather a sincere, hardworking writer with a book you believe in.

Inventing a "one-sentence handle" for yourself will help. Search your background and spell out what makes you qualified to write this book. Imagine that you're writing jacket copy on yourself — what description would make a reader buy and read your work?

In any elaboration, be as specific and succinct and well-organized as possible. Rather than just saying you are uniquely qualified, demonstrate it with names, dates, and sales figures if at all possible. List any books you have published; or if you're a first-time book writer, summarize any other type of credits in a list of the places you've published — magazines (whether local, national, or "little") or newspapers. If an article is particularly noteworthy or relevant to your book, list the title.

If your list of credits, awards, etc., is long, give the highlights or enclose the list separately. If you're indicating your background with a resume, put it on a separate sheet of paper and keep it short. Don't include letters of reference from people unconnected with publishing.

If you've never published anything anywhere, try to come up with a solid reason for your proposed identity as a writer: a writing course; familiarity with current books from reading them as a librarian, teacher, or parent; a strong idea that means a lot to you and that you're convinced would appeal to others.

Tell Ed *only what is necessary to make a decision on your book* — not your life story.

Put your most compelling information first, such as having written a related book, particularly if it has sold well, won an award, been selected by a book club, or gotten a good review you can quote. If you've taught your book's subject or risen to a prominent position within the field, mention that right off. Similarly, if your credits are slim, make that your last paragraph and stress your desire to work hard.

In nonfiction, Ed wants to know your expertise, the special training you've had that uniquely qualifies you to write this book. Ed needs proof that you know what you're talking about and that you're aware of your competition. If it's fiction with a particular locale or background, consider mentioning your related experience, if you have it. If Siberia, mental hospitals, or kiwi fruits are important to your story, you can mention that you lived there, worked in one, or grew them.

Whether it be in fiction or nonfiction, Ed appreciates evidence that you've written "what you know" — not necessarily the minutiae of your life, but what means something to you, what you *want* to know, what you're passionate about. A phrase or a sentence about your passion will, if it's convincing, intrigue Ed.

WHY PAST CREDITS HELP

Ed's *most* important concern is the book that's in front of his or her nose that day, but Ed also wants to think you have a writing career ahead of you, which previous credits help to prove. Ed is not particularly looking for "one-book authors," unless the "one book" is incredibly irresistible.

Previous books or articles tell Ed: "Another editor has read my work and validated it by publishing it." Ed, being overworked and with a tendency to be suspicious of the daily mail, looks for clues that someone else has "vetted" your writing, even if it wasn't necessarily a book editor. This makes you seem less of a total stranger — it's a type of "introduction" to learn that other editorial eyes have passed judgment on you.

(This explains in part why Ed tends to favor material from agents: Ed knows the material has been screened — it's had a reading by at least one publishing professional, been deemed worthy of consideration, and very likely undergone editorial back-and-forth with the agent acting as editor. It's not going straight from someone's printer into Ed's hands. Agent-less books have to convey this same worthiness, by their own strength and the careful mention of credentials.)

Previous credits also protect Ed against unpleasant surprises. They indicate that you understand something about publishing, that you're capable of revision if your book has flaws, because presumably you've revised before. This can be a deciding factor if your book is good but needs work.

FACTS OF LIFE

Once again, don't despair if you seem to lack credentials. When writers write the best books that they can, they can very often lure editors into publishing an "unknown."

A writer with slim credentials, however, will usually have to do more work "on spec" than will an established writer. You'll have to invest more of your time up-front to prove to Ed that you can do the work and to allow Ed to spot major problems right away.

In nonfiction, this frequently means that your proposal must be much more thorough — you may actually want to submit an outline for a book you've already written, which you'll then have to be willing to revise if necessary. In fiction, you *do* need a complete manuscript to sell a book, although you don't want to send any more than the first three chapters and a synopsis until Ed asks to see more. Whether fiction or nonfiction, your writing should speak for itself—if it's necessary to send writing clips from other projects you've done, something is probably wrong.

Doing this much labor without a guarantee it will sell may seem reprehensibly risky. Submitting a book *is* riskier for the new writer, but that's how writers get started. It's the only way Ed can make an informed judgment. Some established writers work this way, too—wanting, for their own satisfaction, to have the whole book complete before getting a publisher interested in it.

Finally, unless Ed has previously indicated an interest in your work, it's somewhat presumptuous to express in your first letter your willingness to promote your book. But Ed, wanting to know if you're energetic, even potentially "tourable," can read between the lines of a well-prepared cover letter. The way you act *now* (enthusiastic, confident, alert, sensitive) will show Ed how you will behave later . . . and will put thoughts of your money-making potential into Ed's head. Read on.

9.

WILL THE BOOK MAKE MONEY?

*Sir, no man but a blockhead ever wrote
except for money.*
　　　　　　　　— Samuel Johnson

If editors have answered "yes" to most questions up till now, they've decided you've got a publishable book. They must now make the leap to believing it *salable*.

And the patron saint of editors isn't called Saint Francis de Sales for nothing. "Acquiring a publishable, salable manuscript is what publishing is all about," writes editor William Targ.

Traditional wisdom says that out of every ten books published, four lose money, three break even, and three make money. Sometimes a book makes a lot of money — but the average profit margin for the average commercial trade publisher is an unspectacular 6 percent to 8 percent.

The *average* hardcover title sells fewer than 5,000 copies and loses money.

Obviously, books that are borderline or merely competent won't necessarily sell — a salable book calls for something special.

Unfortunately, there's a dearth of hard data about that "something special." Successful editors figure it out more often than not, but even they can't always articulate it. Of publisher Phyllis Grann's amazing instinct for spotting bestsellers, for example, one agent says, "There's no telling what it is. But if you could bottle it, you'd make a fortune."

Despite this dearth of data, an editor, writes publisher M. Lincoln Schuster, "must be able to distinguish between black ink and red."

Editors dutifully consult with in-house marketing people

and key sales reps, with bookstore personnel and influential librarians. They prepare elaborate return-on-investment forms, painstaking profit-and-loss statements—and as if they hadn't already bombarded the poor book with enough questions, they now ask some tough ones:

• Will people spend what to them will seem like a lot of money on your book? This is an excellent test of the book's merit. Will the book inspire the key to good sales: word of mouth?

• Does your book meet a need in the marketplace? Is it strong enough to compete in a crowded library market and crowded bookstores?

• Will it sell in nonbook outlets (supermarkets, warehouse clubs, airports, discount stores, hardware stores, toy stores, computer stores, etc.) which is where 25 percent of books are bought by consumers today?

• What is the current *state* of the marketplace, especially for your type of book? Also the economy in general? Can we *afford* to publish this?

• What are the sales figures on your previous books or on your type of book?

• Does your book resemble books that have made—and especially lost—money for us in the past?

• What is the marketing staff's estimate of your first year's sales? Will the initial print run be high enough to justify production costs and impress key booksellers?

• What can we price your book at—and will it leave any profit after costs are figured in?

• Will your book need a particular promotion plan to get it into the hands of buyers, and what will that cost?

• Does your book have limited appeal (New Yorkers, say, or another regional audience), or a national, even universal appeal? How will it sell in Iowa (a state that has the highest rate per capita of books checked out of the library)?

Marketing input is crucial, both now and later. "Even if you feel strongly about a book," says editor Eleanora Schoenbaum, "you don't want to be *alone* with it. You want to see the light build in someone else's eyes, too—and keep that excitement going throughout the life of a project."

Most editors have no desire to make their professional lives any more difficult by signing up a book their sales staff does not like—it's an uphill, pointless battle.

Such a battle, says editor Faith Sale, means trouble getting "enthusiasm from people in other departments which is then conveyed to sales reps and from them to the people who buy from them, and [then] to book reviewers"—a disaster all the way around. Another editor agrees: "Sometimes you learn, only by making the mistake of publishing something which doesn't do well, that it did not truly fit the identity of the company."

HEARING THE SOUND OF MONEY

Ed has no great wish to associate with money-losers. Just the reverse: A book that sounds as if it's going to make money gets a million times more exciting. As writer Jay McInerney handed the last pages of *Bright Lights, Big City* to his editor Gary Fisketjon, the latter is said to have started laughing: "I hear," he said, "the sound of money."

Editors are no different from writers. "No matter what any writer will tell you, we write because of the money," says writer Harold Robbins. "If there was no money, we'd do something else." Another writer who ought to know, James Clavell, feels that writers have to be extremely astute about the market to get paid what they're worth; in Clavell's case, it was a $5,000 advance for his first novel, $7,500 for his second, and on upward to the *$5 million* he received for *Whirlwind*.

Ultimately, even if all marketing questions are answered to an editorial board's satisfaction, *no one really knows* if a book will sell. Even if it's nearly identical to another book, as in a series, the condition of the marketplace could fluctuate.

Market research could be done, but in a low-margin business like publishing, "the first edition of a book *is* the market research," says publisher Clarkson Potter. "It's cheaper to publish the book than to ask somebody if he might want it because he doesn't know the answer until it *is* there."

"I don't sign up a book without giving a lot of thought to the market for that book," says another editor, "but I can't say *exactly* what that market's going to be." If editors knew exactly what books were going to make money, most of them would sign up only sure things—and most writers wouldn't have average incomes just two steps above migrant farm workers'.

Instead, many books fall into the cracks. "You can do everything right," says Gary Fisketjon, "and the book still might not sell." Certainly, editors would dictate what people buy if they could. "We don't *try* to lose money," editor Page Cuddy points out.

Realistically, publishers would therefore be better off banking their money than gambling on your next book—*unless* they feel yours is one of those three that will be written in black ink, not red.

There's no need, however, to get depressed by the list of questions above, because in lieu of or in spite of some of the answers, your friendly editor relies on editorial speculation. "We all like to feel we're involved in the hunch, the occasional risky project, not always playing it safe," says editor Michael Korda. "There ought to be room for the brushfire to catch around something improbable, odd and wonderful once or twice a season."

WHY BESTSELLERS SELL BEST

Most editors play it safe *most* of the time because they know the competition for people's money and time. Book publishing, says one publisher, "is still an industry which, compared to its competition within the leisure field, affects an infinitesimal proportion of the total population. . . . There is something very deep-seated and deep-rooted in our culture which makes most people suspicious of or insensitive to *books*."

Books compete, first of all, with other books. Writes one

bookseller: "If your book is the best you can do and it still does not stand up in competition to the other heavyweights—sorry. I don't want it on my shelf taking up space that could otherwise go to something that would sell and pay the rent."

Also, a book buyer has to make the effort to seek it out and want it badly enough to pay what will seem like a lot of money for it. Books aren't like magazine articles, which are conveniently there for the captive audience that's already purchased the magazine.

Then there's the cost. Instead of a hardcover children's book, a parent could buy a week's worth of diapers. For the price of a hardcover novel, you can go to a couple of museums, see a play or two, or spend a day at an amusement park. You can go see three movies, or rent ten of them for your VCR. Or you can spend nothing and listen to radio or tapes or watch TV, activities with the advantage of letting busy people do other things at the same time.

Institutions (schools and libraries) want their money's worth as much as consumers. Fighting finite budget constraints, institutions want books that last, both in content and physical construction.

To compete, a book first of all has to be a *good book*. "I used to think we could sell anything," says one marketing executive, "but that's not true. The book needs to be good."

Books also have to offer things the buyer can't get elsewhere: more sex than you can get on TV, for instance, or a virtual guarantee of solid entertainment, or beautiful design and artwork, or crucial and well-organized information, or literary value and intimations of immortality and all the other intangibles we writers know and love about books.

Buyers who aren't writers, on the other hand, will take the easiest route and reach for a brand-name author, a series book, or a book already on the bestseller list. "Why Bestsellers Sell Best" reads an appropriate headline to an article explaining why publishers frequently don't advertise a book *until* it's selling already.

Not all genres are affected by the brand-name syndrome. It crops up most often with hardcover fiction. "Most hardcover novels," writes editor Richard Marek, "even literary ones . . . are given as presents, and it is therefore safer for a buyer to purchase a well-known author than an unknown." Admits James Clavell: "The trick is to become a brand name." Even when brand names turn their hand to new areas—e.g., children's books by Clavell, John Jakes, Cleveland Amory, James Herriot; adult books by Judy Blume or Dr. Seuss—they *still* sell.

By comparison, publishing an unknown is a little "like throwing a butterfly into the Grand Canyon and waiting for the echo," says editor James Wade.

FINE LINES AND BOTTOM LINES

Still, as you know, books by comparative unknowns find good homes every month—books that some editor believes will make money, or else are so important for some reason that they should be published anyway.

With such books, Ed may map out elaborate marketing strategies to leave as little to chance as possible, or else will look for signs that you'll one day be more commercial. Paul Theroux's publisher brought out five of his books before *The Great Railway Bazaar*, his first major success. Bernard Malamud published eleven books before reaching fame with *The Fixer*.

"There is no evidence that books of real merit are going unpublished because of 'the bottom line,' " stresses John F. Baker in *Publishers Weekly*.

Almost anyone in publishing—whether it's commercial, small press, university press, regional, reference, specialized, scholarly—would agree. *Publishable books will, with persistence, get published*.

In the fine line Ed walks between being thought a profit-oriented sleaze and a math-hating wimp, Ed will take into account all the questions listed here—and will still find books to believe in and sign up.

HOW TO GET TO THE "YES" ANSWER

Strange but true: *You* have a major role in deciding whether or not your book makes money.

That role will sound familiar: It's researching your publishers—again. If you haven't done this as recommended thus far, perhaps money will provide the necessary impetus.

You need to find the publishers who do a good job with the kind of book you're writing. This may be a small press, a university press, a trade publisher known for elegant literary volumes, one specializing in your subject matter, a house known for its smash bestsellers, one with a distinguished children's book list, etc., etc. Only your research will tell you.

You need to connect with the right editor who will see the money-making potential, literary excellence, or intrinsic importance of your book, and *you*, more than anyone else, have the power to make this connection.

In the bookselling locales you've been inspecting all along (bookstores as well as the increasingly important non-book outlets), study the displays relevant to you, matching books with publishers.

If your goal is to hit the bestseller list, you'll want to inspect your nearest chain bookstore. With titles expected to be commercial successes, the Waldenbooks chain, for instance, takes between 10 percent and 25 percent of the total books printed. In a world where *one out of every nine* trade books is purchased at a Waldenbooks store, it's imperative to analyze the books you find there.

Study writers' magazines and directories to find out who publishes what, if they're still doing it, and the names of the editors who do it. Ask around: Get publisher evaluations from your writing friends and from new acquaintances at writing conferences.

You'll start noticing who *publishes* those authors who get on TV or radio talk shows, or places you envision yourself promoting your book. Study ads, reviews, and bestseller lists—all the while taking notes on the publishers of the books of interest to you.

Detective work on publishers will unearth tidbits of information you can really use. It's greatly to your advantage to ask some tough questions of your own. Which publishers. . .

- have excellent distribution—their books everywhere you

turn around? "The distribution of books, the bringing of the author's work to the public," says consultant Leonard Shatzkin, "is the service for which the author needs the publisher the most."

- market aggressively? get lots of publicity?
- market more subtly—but also effectively?
- seem to do *nothing* for their books? seem to let books drift?
- don't advertise, or advertise only brand names?
- advertise deserving books by unknowns?
- publish books that reviewers can't say enough say wonderful things about, or by authors you admire?
- publish books that reviewers invariably trash?
- do books that never *get* reviewed?
- are associated with this year's Pulitzer or Nobel winners, or winners of prizes and awards in your field?
- are known for sticking with authors from early promise to full-blown success?
- have longevity and status, with editors who see books through from start to finish?
- actively "service" the books they sign up, taking the measures appropriate to wring maximum sales from each?
- are liable to be in business to market your book once it's published?
- publish reasonably priced books?
- publish books priced too high—to the point where it could theoretically cut into sales?

If you're the super-conscientious type, you can check back issues of *Publishers Weekly* for financial status reports on various publishers. Also, if you want to investigate a small press, it's not unheard of to order (through your banker) a Dun & Bradstreet report on its credit rating.

KNOWING YOURSELF

Should you approach the publishers paying the huge advances, with constant bestsellers? Is this the kind of book you're writing? How often do they publish new writers? Would you be better off in the long run with a less commercial house or small press that quietly but effectively gets the kind of book you write to the right audience and does a good job keeping it in print? Only research will tell you.

When researching, it's best to look at the market as it applies to *your* book, and to be honest. "I'm no Joan Didion," says bestselling author Judith Krantz. "I want to be known as a writer of good, entertaining narrative." Says Tom Clancy: "I'm not the new Hemingway, I'm in the entertainment business." Admits James Michener: "I'm not a stylist. There are a whole lot of things I'm not good at. . . .What I can do is put a good narrative together and hold the reader's interest."

Many writers would be just as happy to be Didion or Hemingway—the point is to try to know yourself, and then find out about the editors to whom you would appeal. Editors know themselves, as well. Says one leading commercial editor: "Sure, I'd like to edit Nadine Gordimer or someone like her," but agents and authors don't send that kind of material to an editor known for huge commercial successes.

Savvy writers devote the same kind of serious thought to the marketing of their books as they do to their writing. The two are more closely linked than beginning writers realize. Says consultant Marilyn Ross: "One hopes that the author was thinking marketing from the minute he or she started writing the book." After publication—and in getting Ed to say "yes" in the first place—"Authors' efforts can have a dramatic impact on the sale of their books," stresses Ross.

You can indicate your awareness that the publisher is (at least theoretically) in business to make money by providing your well-chosen editor with as much evidence as you can of your book's salability. (But don't, in your cover letter, tell Ed exactly how much money you're going to make for the company—this amateurishly usurps Ed's role.)

In answering Question #4 about your audience, you'll ideally have identified who you think will pay money for your book. Making your book as solid as you can will justify the average selling price these people will have to pay. If it's nonfiction, for example, emphasize the book's reference value, and plan for useful appendixes and an irresistible table of contents. If it's a children's book, don't assume that a slight idea makes a book.

FINDING A HOME

Finally, it always helps to ask yourself if *you're* truly excited about your own book.

According to author Leonard Felder, "There has to be tremendous excitement in the author"—and even that will fail to grip the editor and hence the publishing company unless "the author has not only written well but created publicity and marketing opportunities the publisher can exploit." The author is responsible for initiating his or her own word of mouth on the book, with the rest of the world taking it from there. And to do this, "Authors must learn the business" of how books are published and sold.

All of this—in addition to writing the best book that you can. It sounds like a very tall order, but it's definitely not impossible, and it makes your writing that much more pleasurable, knowledgeable, and profitable.

Good books do sell. In a survey of booksellers regarding books that were expected to sell but didn't, the comments ran: "The packaging was wonderful; the story didn't seem to work. . . . A terrible book! . . . The customers who bought it hated it and word got around. . . . Poor quality. . . . Just couldn't see the merit in it. . . . It's the stupidest book I ever heard of."

Says one bookseller: "A book that is filled with incredible wonderfulness (highly technical term) will delight the bookseller and sell well because it spreads its joy easily." As translated by a paperback editor: "Good books generally sell better than bad books."

Take the $20 test: Ask yourself if *you'd* spend $20 (or the average price of the type of book you're writing) on your book. As John F. Baker puts it: "Before you curse the next publisher who turns you down, pause to wonder: Would *I* buy a copy of this book I've just sent in? If not, there's your problem, right there."

Is yours a book you would covet for your own shelves?

If the answer is "no," is there anything you can do to make it more salable? How can you shape and craft your material into a must-have for your target audience? What fine-tuning can you do *before* you send your material out?

On the other hand, if the answer is "yes," it's time (at last, at last) to wrap up this phase of your research on publishers and send your book to the editor who's going to agree with you and give it a good home.

NOTE: We now leave the land of the *fairly* familiar and enter the land of what may seem the *totally* strange. Questions 10 through 12 (production, sub-rights, and backlist) deal with matters that editors rightly consider at this point in the submission process, but that may *seem* beyond most beginning (and many experienced) writers' ken and control.

If you've gone through the mill (published at least one book) or know someone who has, the following information should not strike you as particularly intimidating, but rather (ideally) as genuinely helpful in sorting out how editors make their decisions, giving you the keys for taking advantage of this knowledge.

Otherwise, if you're a writer but not yet a published *author*, a word of explanation seems in order: The following three chapters are meant as friendly *information*, not as torment to cause loss of sleep or terminal writer's block. Some writers may find them the most fascinating and useful part of this book, and for those who don't — it's eminently possible to write and sell a book without knowing every detail about production, sub-rights, and backlist. Onward!

PART 3

DESIGN AND PRODUCTION QUESTIONS

10. Can the book be produced economically, in a visually attractive package?

10.

CAN THE BOOK BE PRODUCED ECONOMICALLY, IN A VISUALLY ATTRACTIVE PACKAGE?

Love from people you will never meet!
Love seeping through paper and parch-
ment and ink!

— Erica Jong

Ed now arrives at a make-it-or-break-it decision. Book economics is a function of sales balanced by costs — all of which get tallied up *before* Ed can say "yes" to your book.

Ed likes your book, thinks you've got a good one . . . but learns here whether or not it can be produced economically. Rejection, unfortunately, can occur at this stage — even for perfectly fine books. "It takes a lot of bravery," writes Hugh Rawson, "for an editor to urge an editorial committee to ignore projections that are written in red ink, and no editor . . . wants to be in this position very often."

Knowing how vital a book's physical appearance is to sales, Ed now starts to visualize your book and consult with the designers and the production manager (whose jobs, in some smaller companies, may overlap). Editing, design, and production are the three parts of the bookmaking function, which is *"to transmit the author's message to the reader in the best possible way,"* according to Marshall Lee in his treasure trove of information, *Bookmaking*.

116

Designers help to decide what your book will look like. Production managers decide how much it will all cost.

ROTTEN COVERS, ROTTEN SALES

If the visual people get excited about your book, or conversely, find it dull or banal, this influences Ed's decision.

An enthusiastic designer can transform ordinary manuscript pages into things of beauty, or can make a book look worth a seemingly outrageous cover price. Careful, appropriate packaging proves that the publisher cares for the content—and can be the deciding factor in a buyer's choosing between several books on the same topic (look in the computer section, for instance, and you'll see books with virtually identical titles), or can make a reader buy a book purely on impulse (that snazzy-looking paperback at the counter, for instance).

Some books leave no impression or can even be irritating. "When you put design between the reader and the author," says David Godine, "you violate the basic purpose of a publisher; you're interfering; you're introducing static."

Ed is closely involved in the design process, making sure that your cover is accurate and appealing. The cover is a selling tool—the only advertising most books will ever receive. And books *are* judged by their covers. "Rotten covers mean rotten sales," says one bookstore owner.

Each genre has its own rules, and each publisher has its own quirks. The stylish album-cover looks of many current trade paperback series are thought to be a major factor in selling contemporary fiction by virtual unknowns; "the creepier the better" is the rule in horror book covers. As a consumer, I look for covers I don't mind being seen on an airplane with; an amazing number of books I want to read fail this test.

Ed now thinks about *your* book's visual possibilities:

• Is it easy to visualize what your book will look like: flashy, elegant, lurid, subdued, etc.? Does the unique set of visual variables presented by your book fit in with the publisher's present identity?

• Is it a book that will inspire the design department to go "all out," producing a visual work of art?

• Can an appropriate and economical cover be designed? Is there a scene, theme, character, or conflict that jumps out as good cover material?

• Does the project demand the complicated, the impossible, or the very expensive, in terms of illustration, photos, or layout?

• Does the book present special design problems — as in poetry, cookbooks, art books, the offbeat, etc.?

Visual presentation is more crucial for some books (children's books, coffee table or art books, first novels by unknowns, photo essays, craft books) than for others. But unless it's a specialized company, most editors do not set out to sign up intricate illustrated books, because of the expense and the hassle.

Saying "yes" gets harder when the book is long and complicated, or requires a lot of color photography or illustration, reproductions of famous paintings, or permissions fees and research for photographs. Not only do unusual features lead to an expensive first printing, but they also limit the book's future: A full-color, oversize book may seem like a zippy idea now, but will provoke groans from future staff deciding whether or not it's worth reprinting when reprint costs have escalated skyward.

A borderline book can sometimes get rejected as soon as someone raises the objection: "It's too expensive to produce."

NEVER UNDERESTIMATE THE PRODUCTION MANAGER

A production manager "customarily spends more money in the publishing process than all other departments combined," writes production director David Zable. "We generally spend from one-third to one-half of the total amount spent on a book." Your advance, for instance, is usually a fraction of the cost of your book's paper, printing, and binding.

Unless all costs are standard and predictable (as with an established series), Ed needs a production estimate to prove that your projected sales will justify the always-increasing costs of manufacturing. Ed needs to know:

• Will your book fit easily into an economical size and format that the publisher is accustomed to succeeding with? Are any aesthetic compromises necessary to produce the book economically? Would these harm sales?

• Is it immediately clear what the best format is for your book (hardcover, mass market paperback, trade paperback, etc.), or does it seem ambiguous? In other words, does it clearly belong with this publisher?

• Does Ed foresee any scheduling problems? Is the book so timely that it must be put on a rush schedule, and is this warranted?

• Are any technical difficulties or unusual expenses involved — photo research, permissions fees, maps, charts, graphs, unusual trim size, full-color illustrations, paper engineering, special film work?

• Can you supply camera-ready pages, or use desktop publishing techniques to save money? Assuming the publisher is set up this way (most trade publishers aren't), can you supply your manuscript in disk format compatible with the publisher's computers?

• What size print run would be planned, and is it economical?

• What is the estimated unit cost (see below) of the book, and will this allow the book to be published at a price the market will bear? Does it leave any room for profit?

Ed supplies the production manager with physical specifications for your book: the trim size (width and height of the physical book); number of pages; number and type of illustrations, if any (photos, four-color art, two-color art, line drawings, etc.); type of paper; type of cover (jacket, paper over boards, glossy, embossed, number of colors, etc.); binding (cloth or paper); tentative retail price.

Obviously, Ed has a good idea at this point what your book will look like — and ideally you should, too. All this means is that you need to give Ed an accurate and reasonable estimate of your book's length (a rough word count that Ed can translate into book pages), and information on any special requirements.

The next step is for the production manager to estimate production costs, according to the physical specs above, for copyediting and proofreading; typesetting; design charges; buying art and/or photos for cover and/or insides; film and stripping; proofs and bound galleys; paper; printing; binding; warehousing and shipping; any special expenses.

Fiction is generally easier to estimate because of its standard sizes, standard paper, straightforward typesetting costs, etc. Nonfiction is trickier, with a greater variety in sizes, illustrations, typesetting specs, etc.

The production department gives Ed a "unit cost"—the cost of producing a single copy of your book (a "unit")—down to a fraction of a cent. The higher the print run, the lower the unit cost, because total costs are getting spread out over a greater number of books. If these costs get out of control, or too many books get printed (that don't sell) or too few (driving up the unit cost per book), there is no room for profit.

The realities here can hurt: "While it would seem that people are the most important element in creating a book, it is the printing, the paper, and the binding costs that are," says writer/editor Alice Bach. The cost of paper is always spiraling, for example, and the binding alone is by far the single most expensive element in a hardcover book.

JUGGLING THE NUMBERS

Ed might rethink the project. "No matter how exciting, delightful, and important the editor may think the book is," writes Richard Balkin in giving a useful example of this juggling routine, "if the cost of producing your 900-page full-color illustrated study of the Ojibwa Indians means the house either has to price the book at $59.50 for a first printing of 5,000 copies or sell 35,000 copies at $14.95 just to break even, they probably won't do it." In this instance, the $59.50 would price the book out of its market, whereas a large percentage of the 35,000 would likely end up highly discounted on remainder tables or expensively warehoused somewhere. None of these are possibilities Ed wants to contemplate in signing up a book.

Instead, Ed may try and bring the costs down. Can:

- the book be made shorter or smaller?
- your concept be simplified?
- the number of illustrations be reduced? Can they be printed in one or two colors instead of four?
- some of the unusual expenses be dispensed with?

If Ed can't find ways around the problem or if you won't or can't make changes, it's time for you to move on. Each publisher has its own economics, and the next may see sales potential or production solutions that Ed doesn't.

Part of Ed's job is keeping your book on schedule, which on average means a finished book nine months from the time your manuscript is *accepted* (i.e., not submitted or outlined). Waiting in the wings to produce your book is a fleet of copy editors, typesetters, designers, proofreaders, production managers, camera workers, paper suppliers, printers, and binders, with time frequently scheduled to print your book overseas.

Ed works backward from your publication date — the closer it gets, the more inflexible the schedule — to give you your deadlines. If you start missing yours, everyone gets thrown off. Ed loses face and may resent you, but more important, your book suffers. As Hugh Rawson points out, "Authors who are chronically late in delivering manuscripts should note that dilatoriness reduces the profitability (and publishing appeal) of their books."

Ed wants writers who respect deadlines even in the early stages of a book's acceptance, who know enough basics about design and production to take visual factors into account, who respect the publisher's expertise, and who are realistic about economic limitations.

HOW TO GET TO THE "YES" ANSWER

It's a useful exercise to visualize your book before sending it off. Although this area is considered the publisher's province, troubleshooting your book now can head off some possible reasons for rejection.

If you have trouble visualizing an appropriate look for your book, something is probably wrong. As Richard Balkin points out, "If you don't know approximately how long your book will be, you may not be ready to propose it to a publisher."

Unless you have a special interest in the subject, however, it's not really necessary to learn the whole design and production process in order to sell your book. If you *are* interested, or your book has special requirements you want to educate yourself about before submitting it, good places to start are the relevant chapters in Lee's *Bookmaking*, Marjorie Skillin and Robert Gay's *Words into Type*, *The Chicago Manual of Style*, and Balkin's *A Writer's Guide to Book Publishing*.

ANSWERS TO PREVIOUS QUESTIONS WILL HELP

Meanwhile, what is the state of *your* visual presentation (Question #1)? Is it neat and well-organized, with an ease of reading that sets Ed's mind free to roam far past manuscript pages to visualize a well-designed book?

Always indicate clearly an accurate word count (real or projected), and specify what artwork is included, necessary to obtain, or merely desired.

By studying the format and physical specifications of books in your genre, you can avoid making elementary mistakes. If you're writing a picture book, for example, you wouldn't submit a book that requires thirty-eight pages. (Including front matter, there are thirty-two pages to a picture book, or occasionally forty-eight.) If you're writing a series romance or mystery, do a rough word count of some books (count the words on one or two pages and multiply by the total number of pages) to make sure yours is in the ball park—or, less laboriously, check the acceptable lengths and word counts given in guides such as *Writer's Market*.

It's to your advantage to send editors only what they need

to make a decision, and *no more*. Unless graphics are indispensable to your project, consider dropping them.

Don't send along your own visual material *unless* you're a professional photographer or illustrator. If your text is good and your visuals are amateurish or poorly prepared, Ed is hard put to separate the two and will usually reject the whole project. If photos are essential, send just a few, carefully labeling them and keying them to their specified locations in the text. Take care wrapping and mailing them, and don't ever send originals you haven't duplicated.

Illustrations are not required for submitting a children's book. A strong text can get rejected right along with weak illustrations. Editors are more than capable of visualizing your book (no need to send along stick-figure sketches), and almost always prefer to hire their own artists, for many good reasons summed up by editor Walter Lorraine: "The selection of illustrators has far more facets than most people realize." It helps, however, to have the visuals in the back of your mind at all times, because they do affect your writing—Ed looks for books that inspire thoughts of pictures and artists.

But your sole concern at this point should be to sell your words.

Therefore, you won't want to ask for impossible or exceedingly expensive production or design enhancements, and you might think in advance about what compromises you might be asked to make. The unusual, besides being expensive and making Ed twitch, doesn't always sell. One of the reasons James Dickey's *Alnilam*, for example, supposedly sold poorly—in addition to its difficult title—was that the unusual typography scared readers off. "People picked up the book and put it right back down," said one bookseller.

LETTING YOUR FORMAT FIT YOUR AUDIENCE

Per Question #2, have you taken special care with your beginning? Strange but true: Designers, before translating your thoughts into graphic images, rarely read a whole manuscript, unless it's short (or irresistible). Due to the volume of books designers work on, they have time to read your first few pages, usually your last few, or sometimes just the table of contents.

Your one-sentence handle from Question #3 is what Ed gives designers, along with a description of the audience you've targeted in Question #4. Therefore, you'll want your concept and audience to be immediately clear.

Your answer to Question #4 will be particularly helpful in picturing your format: Let your format fit your audience.

Does your audience, for example, read hardcovers? Will libraries consider your book a must-have acquisition? Is it a book "for the ages," as well as a book consumers will pay upwards of $20 for *right now* (without waiting for the paperback)? Certain types of books, such as business books, are thought to do best in hardcover, and others are a justifiable expense since they'll get used again and again—a classic children's book or a reference book.

People buy hardcovers for the prestige, the newness, the solid respectability. They can be works of art, and are more apt to get reviewed than paperbacks. Many book buyers have paperback-prejudice; *The New Yorker* once said of a book that came out in paperback, "that was right for it, because the story has no heft. . . . You don't read it, exactly—you consume it."

Still, two-thirds of adult books purchased in 1987 were paperbacks (in children's books, the proportions were exactly reversed: Two-thirds were hardcovers). Paperbacks are accessible, affordable, and the preferred choice of teens, college students, and readers of category fiction. Kids who grew up with paperbacks now buy them, and may even find hardcovers intimidating. Trade paperbacks are becoming the preferred mode for original fiction—says editor Gary Fisketjon, "It makes the whole enterprise of publishing fiction a little less hopeless." Staying in print virtually *requires* that a writer be in paperback sooner or later. As editor Rust Hills puts it, "As all writers know now: you're dead if you're not in paper."

The roots of one paperback publisher's success go back to a clerical error that caused the company to print twelve times the number of books it required. The books were nevertheless sold, and the rest is history. Could your book pass this sort of trial by fire? Will it appeal to a very broad readership?

Asking these sorts of questions about your audience can indicate whether you've got a mass-market paperback, a commercial hardcover, a small press volume, a trade paperback. You can, in fact, tip the odds toward getting a "yes" here by picturing one of these formats for your book, researching your publishers to see who is used to producing books in this format, and submitting it to those publishers first.

"It's a little bit like the chicken or the egg riddle," writes John Boswell, "but if you can begin to envision the most appropriate format for your book based on your subject matter, this will be one of your best submission clues later on."

MORE PUBLISHER RESEARCH

If production values are important to your project, you'll want to research your publishers specifically for this factor. Inspect books in your field for weak bindings, cheap paper, badly reproduced illustrations, indications of poor quality control.

Not all books from each publisher are produced with the same consistency, but you'll notice trends. Some publishers pay painstaking attention to a book's production value — acid-free paper, elegant slipcovers, high-quality binding, excellent reproduction of artwork. These publishers, both small presses and larger houses, win awards year after year for their superior bookmaking. Other publishers take shortcuts to make inexpensive books that sell in the millions.

If you're planning a timely book, keyed to a current hot topic or an upcoming event, look for publishers with the capabilities to produce books quickly — not all of them can or want to. Many hardcover publishers, for example, won't take on a project that requires a shorter lead time than nine months from the manuscript's *acceptance* (not submission), even if the potential profit is there. Their publishing mechanisms simply can't respond that quickly.

This fact of publishing life also means that if your book is "a perfect Christmas gift book" or a "sizzling summer read," it actually should be submitted at least *eighteen months* before your target season.

YET MORE RESEARCH

You can make a game out of noticing which of your recent book purchases were influenced by design. Note names of the publishers whose book designs you admire and who you want to work with. Which publishers:

- do an effective job of using the visual presentation as a marketing tool, with designs that are just right for the book's audience, content, and purpose?
- have jackets or covers that are pleasing to your eye, that seduce you, that feel good to the touch?
- make the most of the book's visual possibilities, and publish books that could be considered works of art?
- have books that look too dull to bother with, or that look stupid or ugly—books you'd be embarrassed to be seen with?
- do books that are a pleasure to read—material clearly presented and organized, type that's legible and readable?
- have design disasters: covers that misrepresent the inside in some way, type too small to read comfortably, margins too small (not enough white space), crude illustrations, typos, distracting design elements, a look that makes you uncomfortable for some reason?
- have authors you know (you'll have to ask around) who are happy/unhappy with their jackets?

WHEN TO EXPRESS
YOUR OPINIONS

Once your book *is* accepted, stay in touch. "Ideally, a writer should be involved in his book's production at every stage," says poet/editor Suzanne Zavrian.

But unless you've had years of design training, respect the publisher's expertise. When Ed complains about writers who "meddle," it's because "too often a writer's ideas are quirky, wildly expensive, or technically impossible," says Zavrian.

Avoid the art department's universal complaint: "Everyone's an art director."

Small presses can be more open to a writer's design ideas than commercial publishers, but most editors will at least keep a writer informed. Says agent Elaine Markson: "An editor will show samples of proposed typefaces, paper, and talk over other design particulars, if the writer is interested. And writers should be." Editor George Nicholson agrees: "A lot of author disappointment has to do with a lack of information." *Never be afraid to ask questions.*

Keep Question #6 in mind and fight for the integrity of your book. Watch for misinterpretations, as people enter the scene who might be more concerned with hyping your book's commercial appeal than with accuracy. Get as involved as you can without being a pain in the posterior.

Learning the design stages your book will pass through will tell you how—and when—to phrase visual suggestions. If you have a cover suggestion, for example, make it soon after your book's acceptance, not when the publisher has already commissioned or produced your cover.

You'll want to keep track of your cover—the "dessert the writer looks forward to in the long composing period," says writer Phillip Lopate, "the reward of someone else's creativity fashioning a perfect graphic image for all that you had intended to say; strengthening and protecting the vulnerable inside matter . . . and, withal, embodying the sort of hip design idea you have perceived in the latest covers of Nationally Recognized Names."

Your opinions, based on tact and research, may end up getting overruled by publishing company expertise, but they're worth expressing. You're a book consumer, a theoretical purchaser whose reactions can't be discounted.

More important—especially after you've done the research here—no one knows the content of your book better than you do.

PART 4

SUBSIDIARY RIGHTS QUESTIONS

11. Is the book suitable for films, translation, book clubs, the moon?

11.

IS THE BOOK SUITABLE FOR FILMS, TRANSLATION, BOOK CLUBS, THE MOON?

Publishing houses are addicted to Good News.
— *Phillip Lopate*

Good News is . . . Robert Redford directing an Oscar-winning film out of *Ordinary People*. Philip Glass making an opera out of Doris Lessing's *The Making of the Representative for Planet 8*. Paperback sales that make headlines. TV mini-series that include the author's *name* in the title. After-school specials. Books on tape—currently flying out of stores. Funny French editions of Dr. Seuss. *Winnie-the-Pooh* in Latin. Japanese rights, British rights, German rights. . . . The more progressive book contracts, assuming a successful space shuttle program that will take books out of this world, call for *moon* rights.

"Subsidiary rights" refers to the above Good News—or any sale of the right to use your book in ways other than its original publication, which helps it to reach new audiences.

Ed now consults with the sub-rights staff to estimate your book's sub-rights potential. If the News *is* Good, Ed can get addicted to the mounting excitement. "Publishers are professional optimists," says one publisher, and this works to your advantage.

Ed is still relying on the strength of answers to previous questions—*the book comes first*—but getting no support from sub-rights people here can be bad news for a borderline, "iffy" book.

A book by itself usually has a slim or nonexistent profit

margin, but a book *plus* a promising sub-rights future can make Ed breathe a little easier:

• Harry F. Saint's first novel, *Memoirs of an Invisible Man*, got him a $5,000 advance—and then earned $2.5 million from the sale of film, book club, and foreign rights.

• Tom Clancy, too, got $5,000 for *The Hunt for Red October*, and then went on to sell rights to two book clubs, English rights, and paperback rights to the tune of 4.3 million copies.

• Bret Easton Ellis also got $5,000 for *Less Than Zero*, and then went on to make a killing in paperback and film rights.

• Another $5,000 went to Mario Puzo for *The Godfather*, which sold millions of paperback copies and become the record-breaking film of its time.

• A first short-story collection, *Emperor of the Air* by Ethan Canin, had its paperback rights sold for a record price, plus book club rights and translation rights to nine countries.

• S. E. Hinton's young adult novel, *The Outsiders*, which normally sells 300,000 paperback copies a year, sold one million copies the year the movie of it appeared.

• For some children's books that have been chosen for the PBS "Reading Rainbow" TV series, sales have jumped as much as 900 percent.

• Geraldine Ferraro got $1 million for her autobiography, which the publisher went on to recoup by selling first serial rights, newspaper serialization rights, main selection of Book-of-the-Month Club rights, and English, Australian, and Italian rights.

Not all books have equally spectacular sales, of course, but the ones that make it big, according to a top paperback editor, do so because "the book is terrific, its market easy to identify, its packaging clear and direct." Good books make the difference: In the list of criteria used to select books for the "Reading Rainbow" series, "literary merit" is #1.

SUB-RIGHTS AND THE EDITORIAL EGO

Because sub-rights sales help sell books, they're sometimes a make-it-or-break-it influence on a book's profit and longevity. Also, projected income here can make a book economically viable all by itself—almost regardless of how it sells as a book. On some happy occasions, all the money a publisher has invested in a book can be recovered before a single book is even shipped.

Part of Ed's job is initiating sub-rights activity. Publishers "place more and more emphasis on [editors'] ability to seek out and buy publication and subsidiary rights," according to Thomas Whiteside. Editors have come "to be regarded primarily as acquirers of literary properties rather than as editors per se."

Ed may or may not actually strike the deals, but is involved in making suggestions to the sub-rights staff, wining and dining key purchasers of rights, representing your book at rights conventions, being persistent about looking after your interests.

Most publishers would operate in the red were it not for sub-rights. One major New York publisher claims it "would be destitute without subsidiary rights income." A smaller publisher, in selling its sub-rights, is "out to squeeze seven cents out of every nickel, market the copyright as an asset. On the book itself, we're lucky to squeeze a nickel out for every nickel."

Besides helping cash flow, certain sub-rights sales affect the unit cost bemoaned in Question #10. A book club or foreign rights sale, if timed correctly, significantly lowers the unit cost by raising the size of your first printing—which can make your book suddenly seem feasible.

Then there's the psychological factor: editors seeking a validation of their editorial acumen. A main selection to Book-of-the-Month Club or the Literary Guild can mean an additional 100,000 to 400,000 copies of your book sold. But it also, as editor Richard Marek puts it, "is the first indication to the publisher that an outside, objective, commercial force—not the author, the agent, or the editor's in-house colleagues—has said, 'Yes, this is a good book; we think our subscribers will want to buy it.' "

Sub-rights success can work wonders for Ed's self-esteem and morale — and hence, yours.

SUB-RIGHTS AND YOU

Ed, not being psychic, does not know in advance just what the extent of your success will be. But after much discussion with the sub-rights staff, Ed (who in some small presses may *be* the sub-rights staff) is ready to estimate the various possibilities, assuming your book starts out as a hardcover:

• Will your book work in paperback — does it speak to a wide range of people, and will it still be timely a year or more from now? Is it the type of book that paperback reprinters — either trade or mass market — will fight over, or is it the kind Ed knows from experience they won't touch? Does Ed's company have the capability or see so much potential that they're planning their own paperback edition?

• Does Ed believe in the book strongly enough to submit it to the rigorous review of the major or numerous smaller book clubs? "I love those book club readers," says editor Thomas Congdon, "and I think about them when I acquire a book."

• Will the book be able to cross the ocean to Great Britain and Europe? Does it have universal appeal, or is it strictly an American book?

• Is it suitable for TV or films? In the words of one agent: "Does it have dramatic content? Does it have a sufficient amount of action? [Or] is it an introspective book?" Says one studio executive: "We don't buy very much, so when we do buy, it really has to be special. . . . It's usually the story, the dramatic content, the characters, the uniqueness of the situation." A unique or fascinating locale helps, too. According to a TV executive, "We're usually looking, as anybody else, for something that is very fresh . . . [the book] that stands out as being somewhat unusual."

• Will magazines or newspapers want to excerpt your work?

Either before its publication (first serial rights) or afterward (second serial rights)?

• Could your book be made into an opera, a musical, or a radio show?

• Is there any possibility of merchandise deriving from your book—calendars, T-shirts, greeting cards, mugs, toys, board games, etc.—or licensing of your characters for comics, cartoons, TV shows, etc.?

• Are parts of your book likely to be anthologized, for which permissions fees can be charged? Would any part of your book work as a textbook or an educational filmstrip?

• Could your book be sold in a condensed or abridged version, or as a limited edition? Will a direct-mail company be interested in selling your book through the mail? Would any companies be interested in offering it as a premium?

• Will your book be appropriate for technologies relatively new or to be developed in the future—audio and video cassettes, cable TV programming, software packages, etc.? And what about the moon?

As editors read your material, they have in the back of their minds the criteria for these different markets. Ed may even suggest changes in your proposed book that will increase the likelihood of meeting these criteria later—and may possibly make these changes a condition of your book's acceptance.

The glitzy world of sub-rights, however, is not the ultimate consideration. Your book *as a book* is still primary in the decision-making process that Ed, who works in the *book* publishing business, is working through.

"The minute you get greedy," says small press publisher Bruce McPherson, "and don't publish out of an assessment of its real value *as* a book, you jeopardize the whole apple cart." What happens once that assessment is made is, as they say, icing on your cake.

HOW TO GET TO THE
"YES" ANSWER

Taking a little time to think about your book in terms of other markets—its viability as a paperback or its ability to cross the ocean—can often help you spot ways to make your book stronger *as a book.*

To do this, it helps to stay on top of trends in various media and learn what you can about their criteria for buying rights to your kind of book:

• If you're interested in movies and TV, the best source of information is *Variety*, the weekly newspaper of the entertainment business.

• With book clubs, study ads for the clubs that interest you and note what their selections have in common.

• Take a closer look at your newspapers and magazines—what book excerpts do they run? Would your book appeal to the same audience?

• What kind of books are being recorded now in cassette form? Are the criteria for a "good listen" different from those for a "good read?"

You can use information gleaned from alert media-watching to consider making changes in your book now.

Your concern is to sell your book, however, not to tell Ed you want Robert Redford to direct your movie.

It's a good idea, in fact, to be realistic, if not pessimistic, about future "icing on your cake." Not that many books are actually optioned for the movies or TV, for example, and of the options that *are* bought, 90 percent are never exercised (i.e., the projects never get off the ground). Sub-rights is a "highly volatile industry," in the words of one top sub-rights director. "A book can be on someone's shelf for a very long time and then suddenly become an active property."

Usually, you'll have to sell your book on its own merits—because that's how it will be bought.

"A GOOD TITLE CAN MAKE A SALE"

The thought you gave to making your title come alive for Question #2 will pay off here, too.

"Titles are extremely important, and they can make a big difference," writes editor Bebe Willoughby. In children's books, a paperback editor "might take a novel just because she likes the title and knows kids will respond to it."

"A good title can make a sale," agrees movie producer Frank Doelger. In seeking approval from studio executives to make a film from a book, he adds, "If you go in with a great title and a great one-line plot description, lots of times they won't even bother reading the book."

People purchasing sub-rights do not actually read the stacks of books that come to them—unless they're grabbed by an immediate interest in the book's setting or location, plot, or theme, any of which must be in relatively easy-to-digest capsule form.

Therefore, the one-sentence handle you labored over for Question #3 will be equally essential here. If you realistically assume that it's going to get garbled as it passes from person to person, you'll want to make your handle as clear as possible.

BEING IN TUNE WITH THE TIMES

For Question #4, you started becoming a scholar of the publishers you wanted to work with. Here you'll want to research publishers who market sub-rights aggressively, and submit your book accordingly.

Excellent places to begin are Paul Nathan's weekly "Rights" column in *Publishers Weekly*, wherein all the latest hot deals are detailed, and the "Literati" column in *Variety*.

(According to a recent Paul Nathan column, for instance, "An increasing number of today's [paperback] reprint auctions are for books from small or specialized presses.")

Notice which publishers' names keep coming up, which ones make clever or appropriate deals, actively "squeezing every nickel" out of their books. It's also not unheard of to make your first contact with an editor through a sub-rights person you've read about.

Unless you have some real expertise or connections, mentioning in your cover letter the sub-rights potential you see in your own book looks amateurish. The time to tell Ed the possibilities you see is after your book is accepted. (Generally, the smaller the press, the more likely it is you might think of possibilities the publisher hasn't considered.)

With a good cover letter, however, Ed can read between the lines. Previous sub-rights sales, even the most minor ones, are naturally of most interest. Your credentials, e.g., magazine credits, can tell Ed whether you have first-serial connections.

Most of all, if you're in tune with the spirit of the times as expressed through the various media, your book will speak for itself.

PART 5

YOUR BOOK'S FUTURE

12. Will the book survive on the backlist?

12.

WILL THE BOOK SURVIVE ON THE BACKLIST?

A person who publishes a book willfully appears before the populace with his pants down. If it is a good book nothing can hurt him. If it is a bad book, nothing can help him.
— *Edna St. Vincent Millay*

Your book, on publication day, is a "frontlist" title: It's in the publisher's current catalog, being actively promoted, and easy to order. But after six months, a new crop of frontlist books springs forth from every publisher, and your title becomes "backlist." It might sell for another year, reprinted once or twice, or it can disappear once the first printing has been exhausted.

Or—the publisher can judge the demand for your book high enough to keep reprinting it, season after season. Your book can go on selling almost indefinitely, kept in stock and continuing your royalty income—as well as your satisfaction at having written a book with lasting value. You've proven that the written word is immortal, or at least highly durable. "The oldest books are still only just out to those who have not read them," as Samuel Butler puts it.

Signing up a backlist survivor is the dream of every editor, who'd like to be responsible for creating long-lasting books that make a difference—plus supply a constant source of revenue to the company.

A well-tended backlist accounts for between 50 percent and

90 percent of a publisher's income at any given time, depending on the company. "The life's blood of a publishing house is the backlist," says publisher Roger Straus. Which means that editors, as publisher M. Lincoln Schuster instructs, should look "to the long-life 'survival value' of a given book for your backlist — a criterion far more crucial than immediate sales appeal."

Ed, in evaluating *your* book, may even deem backlist potential as its strongest feature, particularly if it's "iffy" in other respects. "The argument that publishers' backlists are rich in works that sold slowly at first but have continued over time," says editor Jonathan Galassi, "has been used again and again to convince a reluctant publisher to take on a chancy book."

YOU AND THE BACKLIST

Writers submitting a book owe it to themselves to know something about what makes a good backlist title. It might seem that getting "yes" answers to the previous eleven questions would guarantee a "yes" here, but actually, Ed needs to know still more:

• Is yours just such a good book of its kind that it's *bound* to last?

• Have you caught the spirit of the times in a way that's likely to endure? Could you be called a "spokesperson" for your generation? Is it possible you or your book will develop a cult following?

• How likely is your book to remain popular in years to come? Editors look for the fresh and original, but a book that's *too* topical has no future.

• Is your book part of or the beginning of an ongoing series? Demand for one book in a series can create demand for the others. (This can work in reverse, too: A poor-selling series book can drag the others down with it.)

• Do you have other in-print books with the same publisher? Ed is more likely to keep all of your work in print.

• Is this a strong holiday book that could get marketed anew every year — a "Christmas classic" or good Halloween book (Halloween, in particular, being the holiday that sells the most children's books), etc.?

• Is it an inspirational book with timeless, universal appeal?

• If it's nonfiction: With updates as necessary, will the information be useful for some time to come? Does the book have solid reference value that buyers can't get elsewhere?

• Does it tie in to an organization or audience that continually regenerates itself, e.g., children, job-hunters, travelers, Weight Watchers, Alcoholics Anonymous, Girl Scouts, do-it-yourselfers, people seeking medical or sexual advice, new home buyers, bird-watchers, etc.?

• Is your book likely to get on bestseller lists, keeping in mind that "the best way to get a book on the bestseller list is to have written a previous bestseller," according to *The New York Times*. Adds Daniel J. Boorstin: "A 'bestseller' . . . is known primarily (sometimes exclusively) for its well-knownness."

• Will it generate controversy or enormous amounts of publicity? Will people pay money to see what all the fuss is about?

• Do you have the stamina and personality to keep drawing people into bookstores (see Question #8)?

• Is this a book that's groundbreaking or revolutionary in some way? One reason books are *published*, says publisher Richard Snyder, is to bring about change: "Books make people think, they challenge points of view and stimulate change in our social structure." Many publishers, says Jonathan Galassi, "feel in some visceral way that the publishing of significant books is the real purpose of their work."

• Is it likely to face censorship or be banned? This may decrease sales among certain segments of the population while increasing them in others.

• Is there *any* possibility it will provoke a lawsuit? Is it on such shaky legal ground (see Question #6) that the publisher will have to recall the book, either temporarily or permanently?

• Is the book unique in some physical way that will cause prohibitively high reprint costs (Question #10)?

• Will it meet the standards of reviewers? Getting good reviews right away can be especially crucial for a "marginal" book. Getting a starred, boxed, or full-page review (depending on the magazine's policy) is even better. Do you have famous friends who will contribute advance blurbs?

• What are reviewers likely to criticize? Reviews may be the most thoughtful comments your book has gotten since its initial reader's report — Ed pays heed. Reviewers are often the first people (besides Ed) to read your book all the way through.

• Do you have a potentially award-winning book? Major or minor awards, national or regional — any annual "Best Of" lists or special recognition that will set it apart from the thousands of other books published the same year? In children's books, winning a Newbery Medal (for most distinguished contribution to children's literature) is a virtual lifetime guarantee of staying in print; many smaller awards can have similar results.

• Is your book likely to go into a paperback edition (without which it will probably not survive)? Any book club or other major sub-rights deals predicted? Certain sub-rights activity (e.g., the selection of a children's book for PBS's "Reading Rainbow" program) can put an O.P. book back *in* print.

• Is your book of the type that could get "canonized" — entering the literary canon that's taught or anthologized in college or high school courses year after year? Are you one of the increasing number of living writers being deemed "classic" by the literary establishment, women's and minority studies groups, nature writers, special interest groups in your field?

As with predicting sales, *no one really knows* what a book's fate will be, but these are some of the factors that can sway Ed's judgment now.

THE STRUGGLE TO KEEP BOOKS IN PRINT

Editorial egos want more than anything to sign up books that get a good reception and reflect well on the signer-upper. A glowing review can make Ed's week; my feet weren't touching the ground the day I walked up to a prestigious bookstore far from home and saw that three out of the ten books in the window were ones I had signed up and edited.

Good reviews can help keep books in print. Thus, if Ed likes some aspects of your work, but, being an avid student of reviews (even knowing many reviewers personally), can foresee that your book is going to get strong criticism in the reviews, this can hurt your chances.

On the other hand, the common wisdom is that *no* reviews are worse than *bad* reviews. In some fields, bad reviews may actually help sales. "If I get people really screaming about the book," says author Tama Janowitz, "it's more to my advantage than a boring review saying, 'Oh, this is just lovely'. . . . I don't care what people say. I just want them to buy the book." Several bestselling authors are simply immune to bad reviews. Even in children's books, where reviews are normally crucial, at least one author—Judy Blume, arguably the most popular author with actual children—receives modest to poor reviews.

Reviews don't always stand the test of time, either. (See Bill Henderson's whole collection of famous off-the-mark reviews, *Rotten Reviews: A Literary Companion*.)

Still, good reviews in the right publications will lead to paperback reprints, affect bookstore displays, make a book more attractive to film and TV producers, and influence how much advertising money the publisher spends. Single reviews in influential publications have been known to put books onto bestseller lists. "Advertising works if a book is good and the reviews are good," says editor Ashbel Green. "If you don't have those, it doesn't matter."

It's word of mouth, not advertising alone, that sells books and keeps them in print, and word of mouth relates to *good books*. "The decisive factor turns out to be the quality of the writing after all," says editor Connie Epstein.

As Ed is keenly aware, keeping books in print is a constant struggle in an age when most books have "a shelf life somewhere between butter and yogurt," as Calvin Trillin puts it. Several forces conspire to put books out of print too quickly. In most chain bookstores, for example, a paperback that's not selling goes back to the publisher within two months; hardcovers get somewhat longer to prove themselves. Books either flash into bestsellerdom or die a quick death.

Meanwhile, back at the editorial office, editors, in doing their part to fight this boom-or-bust syndrome, look for books *worthy* of keeping alive on the backlist—*good books* (see Question #1) that will last.

HOW TO GET TO THE "YES" ANSWER

A savvy writer thinks "backlist" when determining which publishers to work with and even what kind of books to write. You may find it frustrating breaking into print in the first place, but established writers will tell you there's an even worse hell: watching books in their prime go out of print because the publisher fails to reprint them.

"The prudent author will do some sleuthing," writes editor Hugh Rawson, "to find out how well his or her prospective publisher handles the reprint decision." Ask these questions:

• Do your target publishers *have* healthy backlists—or do they routinely put books out of print quickly? Read and ask around about their reprint policies. What percentage of their profits derive from backlist? Do they have a good backlist catalog? This you can write for.

• Ask a bookseller or two their opinions of your publishers' reprint policies—you're likely to provoke impassioned responses.

• Ask your writing friends about their experiences. Are they satisfied or unhappy with their sales histories?

• How do the publishers treat their authors? Are even their

dead authors kept alive and in print? Which publishers keep books in print even at great sacrifice, e.g., when they're obviously losing money but they think highly of the author?

• Analyze your own experiences lately. Have you ever looked for or tried to order relatively new books only to be told they were O.P.? Which publishers were involved?

• Which publishers have a reputation for publishing books well, knowing their niche and cultivating it? They maintain strong, ongoing relationships with their authors. Their books get reviewed regularly and well.

• Which publishers are more passive, haphazard, or inefficient? Which focus only on forthcoming books, and "benignly neglect" the others?

• Which publishers *fight* for their books? Says one top editor, "It's the publisher's duty to get as much attention for its books as possible," and for her that includes nagging major reviewers who don't get around to her books fast enough. I know one distinguished editor who sits in on awards committees where editors are allowed to attend (but not permitted to make a sound) and *glares* at the speakers when her books come up for discussion. I'm not saying the committee members bow to pressure tactics, but they definitely notice. (P.S. This editor's books win a *lot* of awards.)

• Which publishers consistently win awards and are known for the editorial strength and expertise that helps create books that last? Writers "want a little bit of posterity now," says editor Sol Stein, and can look for editors who will help.

YOUR ROLE

You play an active role in your own backlist success by:
• thinking marketing from the beginning
• coming up with sales ideas and ways to get publicity
• forming your own game plan for who or what publications might review your book

- identifying local TV/radio stations where you can be interviewed and conferences where you can be promoted
- doing whatever it takes to establish yourself and gain credibility

"Clearly, authors must learn the [publishing] business so their suggestions will be realistic and correctly timed," says writer Leonard Felder.

Yes, this is work. "I know, I know, that's *their* job," sympathizes consultant Marilyn Ross. "But you're the one who really suffers when the book doesn't receive an appropriate send-off and quickly goes out of print." Starting to think in these future terms will help you get a "yes" from Ed now.

THE SMALL PRESS ADVANTAGE

Writers concerned about backlist should especially research small presses, independent publishers, and university presses. "We will only publish," says feminist publisher Florence Howe, "if we think that . . . thirty years from now, that book indeed deserves to remain on the list."

Normally, small presses do not deal in bestseller material and are therefore immune to the boom-or-bust plague of more commercial houses. Just the opposite: "Books from smaller firms often sell better and better as they get older," according to consultant Judith Appelbaum.

"We're not interested in books that sell gangbusters for one or two printings," says Down East editor Leon Ballon. "Our books sell for five or six years or more." A regional publisher agrees: "We want . . . books that will last seven years." Another says, "Fundamentally, I'm a backlist publisher."

Small presses tend to be more persistent about identifying and marketing to a specific audience, often with related books, which strengthens the sales of individual titles.

And small presses are more apt to keep a book in print even if it's not selling at the moment. "We couldn't abandon one of our kids," says John Cassidy of Klutz Press.

THE BEST AREAS
FOR LONGEVITY

Besides researching your publishers, it helps to analyze your book in terms of the likeliest backlist categories: Will you have sequels or can you make a series out of it? Would it work as a strong holiday title?

Consider children's books, which usually have a longer shelf life than adult books. The sales curve of the two types of books are very different: Most adult books are frontlist-oriented, peaking in sales within six months after publication, with an immediate drop-off. This peak can bring great profit, but books that don't quickly realize that potential go O.P.

Children's books, by contrast, sell in steadily greater quantities, with a sales peak some *eighteen months* after publication (library buyers base decisions on reviews, which are often slow in coming out), followed by a gentle, gradual decline, sometimes lasting years. Most children's book publishers keep new books in print a minimum of three to five years, and often much longer. "The building of a career in children's books is a slower process," says editor George Nicholson, "but one that is nevertheless successful because the books stay in print much longer."

Perhaps Tolstoy was anticipating this contrast when he wrote: "To compose a fairy tale, a touching little song, a lullaby, an entertaining riddle, an amusing jest, or to draw a sketch which will delight dozens of generations or millions of children and adults, is incomparably more important and more fruitful than to compose a novel . . . which will divert some members of the wealthy classes for a short time and then be forever forgotten."

For longevity, also consider science fiction. "Science fiction novels sell continuously over long periods of time," says SF editor Beth Meacham. "It's not unusual for a science fiction book to be in print continuously for forty years"—even though SF is seldom reviewed by the literary establishment.

Science fiction (as well as romances and children's books) is also known as a field where unsolicited manuscripts are considered more carefully.

TAKING YOUR TIME

Whatever your chosen field, the *most* important action is to make your book as solid as possible, writing the best book you're capable of. "When it comes to building a career," writes editor Bebe Willoughby, "almost everything is based on the strength of the book."

If you stay on top of current reviews, awards, and bestseller lists, you can almost start anticipating your own critical reception. Start with *Publishers Weekly, The New York Times Book Review, Library Journal, Booklist,* and *Kirkus Reviews,* all available at your library. Figuring out the standards of awards committees will benefit you now in selling your book. And you can learn a tremendous amount by keeping up with reviews, which will often stimulate new ideas and the motivation of "I could write a better book than what's being published now," the inspiration behind many fine books.

You can do your own research into what publications would be likely to review your book, and what awards and contests your book may be eligible for (and their deadlines and requirements). The smaller the publisher, the more this information will come in handy later. But even a large house will not automatically consider all the avenues you, in your enthusiasm, will discover.

Read books in your field, your competition, reference guides for writers, directories like *Writer's Market* and *Literary Market Place,* newsletters from writers' organizations, and whatever seems related to your book. You'll be absorbing current standards and trends, and you'll be establishing yourself as a member of the literary community.

"Read, read, read," writes William Faulkner. "Read everything — trash, classics, good and bad, and see how they do it. . . . Read! You'll absorb it. Then write. If it is good, you'll find out. If it's not, throw it out the window."

(If it's good, send it to your target editor. If it's not, don't.)

"Take your time," adds Jack London. "Study the stuff of other fellows who've mastered the trick — study until you can turn the same trick. Take your time; elaborate; omit; draw; develop. . . . And take your time."

If you take the time to apply all twelve of these keys to your book, you'll have done the homework a writer needs to do to write a good book that will sell, and ideally, endure.

A QUIZ, SOME FAMOUS REJECTION STORIES, AND SOME ENCOURAGING WORDS

. . . of making many books there is no end.
—Ecclesiastes 12:12

"How does anything ever get published?" might be the logical, screaming response to the torrent of perfectionist sentiments you've been reading.

As of this writing, however, the book publishing business is astoundingly healthy, with activity flourishing everywhere (especially in children's books and at small and university presses), and nothing but good forecasts to come. In my fifteen years as an editor, I *know* that a publishable book will get published, and in doing the research for this book, I kept running into the same theme: Writers who are serious about their work will always get published.

This takes, as you can tell, some genuine work. All established writers (unless they're of the "never-let-them-see-you-sweat" variety) will agree: There are no quick and dirty routes to getting published. Writers must work on their ideas, work on their prose, and then work at finding out about the real world of publishing.

Also, it's perfectly obvious that not every book being published meets all the idealistic criteria in the ideal world of this book. Yes, bad books get published, too.

Editors frequently settle for less, for a variety of reasons, often because they have to. "The majority of what gets into print in the end is ephemeral and mediocre," writes one fiction editor, "done to fill slots in the distribution system, to keep the sales force busy and the voracious readership, if not fully satisfied, at least somewhat entertained, and to maintain the authors as they build up to masterpieces planned or hoped for."

Ignoring editorial criteria, however, tends to get a beginner in the publishing world nowhere fast. For the beginning writer, knowledge of the keys to how editors think is crucial to getting published faster. It's simply a fact of life that a new writer must try harder to meet these criteria, until they become second nature — which they will.

Take a quiz and test your book according to these twelve keys. (Hint: The one correct answer to each question is a virtual quote from the relevant chapter.)

1. Is yours a *good book*, or does it have that potential?
   a) You can talk about your topic better than you can write about it.
   b) You've addressed your package to a living editor you know shares your interests.
   c) You know you have a good idea, once an editor cleans up the writing.
2. Does your book come alive?
   a) The editor requires chemical stimulants to get through the book.
   b) The best sentence in your book is your 243rd.
   c) It makes the editor want to skip lunch, dinner, and sex to finish reading it.
3. Does your book have a clearly defined focus?
   a) It takes the editor an hour to explain your book to someone.
   b) In your cover letter you concisely sum up your book in one sentence.
   c) Staying out of bookstores has helped you focus.
4. Does your book have a clearly defined audience?
   a) You supply the editor with statistics on the number of people who buy your type of book.
   b) You send your book to every publisher whose name begins with A.

    c) Your book has an audience of two—you and your mother.

5. Is your book original and fresh?
    a) Your book resembles a well-publicized bomb on last year's list.
    b) The best way to get published is to write the kind of book that's already glutting the market.
    c) You've thoroughly checked *Books in Print* for competing books.

6. Does your book have integrity?
    a) You libel living editors.
    b) You feel a responsibility to your readers to get things right.
    c) You feel the editor's job is to correct grammar.

7. How much editorial work will your book require?
    a) You feel only amateurs rewrite their work.
    b) Editors, if they don't want your work, will always tell you how to revise it.
    c) Your book shows clear evidence of how seriously you take your writing.

8. What are your credentials for writing this book?
    a) You dedicated your book to the editor.
    b) Your credentials make up for lack of talent.
    c) You've indicated why you're uniquely qualified to write this book.

9. Will your book make money?
    a) You don't care.
    b) Your book would make money no matter which publisher you sent it to.
    c) You'd pay money for your book if it were written by someone else.

10. Can your book be produced economically, in a visually attractive package?
    a) You've spilled coffee or wine on your manuscript to increase its visual appeal.
    b) Envisioning the audience for your book has helped you envision its format.
    c) You lack artistic skill but send along a cover drawing anyway.

11. Is your book suitable for films, translation, book clubs, the moon?
    a) Your title is so clever that it takes a few minutes to realize what it means.
    b) You ask if Bill Murray can play your hero in the movie.
    c) Your first priority is to make your book as strong as possible.
12. Will your book survive on the backlist?
    a) The audience for your book will continually regenerate itself.
    b) Backlist sales are not important to a writer's income.
    c) You don't know if your publisher has a backlist.

FAMOUS REJECTION STORIES

In learning what editors look for, you have seen the importance of publisher research, and how the maddening stock phrase "not right for our list" actually has meaning. You've seen that the phrase contains "a lot of collective experience, intelligent guesswork, and honest admission of incapability to see the right way to publish the book," as editors James Wade and Richard Marek write. And you've seen that learning a few basics about editors doesn't have to take long or absorb attention that's more properly given to one's writing.

What this boils down to is that if you have a good book, you must *keep trying* until you find, through research, the list it *is* right for.

Many, many writers before you have succeeded in just this way, and it will be of comfort to know there *is* light at the end of the submission tunnel—and for many writers, a lot of light:

• Madeleine L'Engle's *A Wrinkle in Time* was published after twenty-six rejections and went on to win the Newbery Medal, currently ranking as one of the top ten trade paperback bestsellers of all time.

• Beatrix Potter after seven rejections published *The Tale of Peter Rabbit* herself—whereupon one of the rejecting publishers changed its mind and is still selling the book eighty years later.

• Donald J. Sobol, who as the creator of the "Encyclopedia Brown" series receives 2,000 fan letters a year, was rejected by twenty-six publishers during the two years it took him to sell his first book.

• Grace Metalious' *Peyton Place* had fourteen rejections before its success.

• Roger Tory Peterson's classic *Field Guide to the Birds* had five.

• Irving Stone's *Lust for Life* endured seventeen rejections before it went on to sell 25 million copies.

• James Michener's first publisher turned down *Tales of the South Pacific* until he'd sold two of the tales to magazines on his own. The book went on to win the Pulitzer Prize and get adapted as the musical, "South Pacific."

• Robert W. Pirsig's cult classic, *Zen and the Art of Motorcycle Maintenance*, was rejected 121 times.

• Leo Buscaglia was writing for twenty years before he gained an acceptance.

• Brian Moore's *The Lonely Passion of Judith Hearne* was rejected by twelve American publishers before being published in England.

• Vladimir Nabokov's *Lolita* was rejected by four major New York publishers before being published first in France.

• Astrid Lindgren, now Sweden's most widely read author, endured rejection of her first *Pippi Longstocking* book.

• Judy Delton persisted through twenty-seven rejections of what became *My Mom Hates Me in January*.

• Ursula LeGuin submitted novels for eleven years without an acceptance.

• William Kennedy's *Ironweed* gathered thirteen rejections before it won acclaim and the Pulitzer Prize.

● Norman Mailer's *The Naked and the Dead* endured nearly a dozen rejections.

● Betty Smith's classic, *A Tree Grows in Brooklyn*, was turned down ten times.

The list of regrettable rejections (for many reasons, including editors asleep at the wheel) is endless. Persistence, obviously, is one factor in getting published. The main difference between the writers above and writers who don't get published is often a capacity for dealing with rejection. Some writers can pick themselves up after a failure and go on to succeed, and some can't.

Evaluating your book in terms of the key questions editors ask is another factor. Think like an editor, and you *will* eventually succeed.

(Answers to Quiz: 1-b, 2-c, 3-b, 4-a, 5-c, 6-b, 7-c, 8-c, 9-c, 10-b, 11-c, 12-a.)

ANNOTATED
BIBLIOGRAPHY

American Society of Journalists and Authors Staff. *The ASJA Handbook: A Writer's Guide to Ethical and Economic Issues.* American Society of Journalists and Authors, 1985. (*Question #6.*)

Appelbaum, Judith and Nancy Evans. *How to Get Happily Published: A Complete and Candid Guide.* Harper & Row, 1982. (*Helpful for all aspects of selling your book, especially what happens afterward — the "happily" part.*)

Authors Guild Bulletin. 234 West 44th Street, New York, NY 10036. (*Writers need book publishing credits to join the Authors Guild; otherwise, try to get a published friend to share the bulletin — invaluable for current information on editors.*)

Balkin, Richard. *A Writer's Guide to Book Publishing.* Hawthorn, 1981. (*Comprehensive reference guide to questions writers ask editors.*)

Bell, Herbert W. *How to Get Your Book Published.* Writer's Digest Books, 1985. (*Overview of the publishing process as it applies to writers.*)

Berg, A. Scott. *Max Perkins: Editor of Genius.* Dutton, 1978. (*Enjoyable and scholarly biography of the legendary editor.*)

Bernstein, Theodore M. *The Careful Writer: A Modern Guide to English Usage*. Atheneum, 1965. (*Question #1: Alphabetically organized, entertaining handbook by a former* New York Times *editor.*)

Block, Lawrence. *Telling Lies for Fun and Profit: A Manual for Fiction Writers*. Arbor House, 1981. (*Questions #1, 2, 5, 6: A truly useful book on all aspects of writing novels — including titles, beginnings, creating a series, creative plagiarism, and what editors want: the same only different.*)

Books in Print. R. R. Bowker, annual. (*Question #5: A necessity for checking your competition.*)

Boswell, John. *The Awful Truth About Publishing*. Warner Books, 1986. (*Subtitled* Why They Always Reject Your Manuscript & What You Can Do about It, *this offers solid information on Questions #3 and 4 and the nuts and bolts of book proposals and queries.*)

Brohaugh, William. *Professional Etiquette for Writers*. Writer's Digest Books, 1986. (Writer's Basic Bookshelf) (*Question #6: How to act around editors and get treated as a professional, before and during the book sale. Recommended.*)

Brown, Rita Mae. *Starting from Scratch: A Different Kind of Writers' Manual*. Bantam, 1988. (Everything *on the writer's life, from what to read and how to use language to what to eat and drink and how to know what a publisher can and can't do for you.*)

Buchman, Dian D., and Seli Groves. *The Writer's Digest Guide to Manuscript Formats*. Writer's Digest Books, 1987. (*A whole book on manuscript preparation.*)

Cerf, Bennett. *At Random: The Reminiscences of Bennett Cerf*. Random House, 1977. (*Random House editors at work.*)

The Chicago Manual of Style, 13th ed. University of Chicago Press, 1982. (*Question #1: Most publishers' editorial style is based on this classic reference book on grammar and style; more scholarly than* Words into Type.)

Collier, Oscar, with Frances S. Leighton. *How to Write and Sell*

Your First Novel. Writer's Digest Books, 1986. (*Question #1: Specific advice on crafting novels, complete with seventeen case histories of successful novelists.*)

Commins, Dorothy. *What Is an Editor? Saxe Commins at Work.* The University of Chicago Press, 1978. (*Biography of editor who worked with William Faulkner, Eugene O'Neill, Isak Dinesen, Dr. Seuss, and many others.*)

Cool, Lisa. *How to Write Irresistible Query Letters.* Writer's Digest Books, 1987. (Writer's Basic Bookshelf) (*Questions #1, 2, 8: A whole book on how to get an editor's attention.*)

Delton, Judy. *The 29 Most Common Writing Mistakes and How to Avoid Them.* Writer's Digest Books, 1985. (Writer's Basic Bookshelf) (*Question #1: A companion to Strunk and White — the writing flaws that cause editors to reject books.*)

Dessauer, John. *Book Publishing: What It Is, What It Does.* R. R. Bowker, 1981. (*Solid overview of publishing; see Chapter 3, "How Books Are Created."*)

Fulton, Len, ed. *The International Directory of Little Magazines and Small Presses.* Dustbooks/Pushcart Press/W. W. Norton, annual. (*Essential for publisher research on small presses.*)

Gardner, John. *The Art of Fiction: Notes on Craft for Young Writers.* Knopf, 1984. (*Question #1: Theory and exercises for the serious beginning writer of fiction.*)

Gill, Brendan. *Here at the New Yorker.* Random House, 1975. (*"Behind closed doors" with some of the most influential editors ever.*)

Gross, Gerald, ed. *Editors on Editing: An Inside View of What Editors Really Do.* Harper & Row, 1985. (*The best book for anyone who wants to know what editors do all day — over twenty-five editors talk about their craft. It's also worth looking up the 1962 edition, which contained some gems.*)

Henderson, Bruce. *How to Bulletproof Your Manuscript.* Writer's Digest Books, 1986. (Writer's Basic Bookshelf) (*Question #6: Protecting yourself against legal action at every stage of writing a book, whether fiction or nonfiction.*)

Horowitz, Lois. *A Writer's Guide to Research*. Writer's Digest Books, 1986. (Writer's Basic Bookshelf) (*Questions #1, 2, 4, 6: Invaluable help for getting the latest information for your book and on your audience.*)

Larsen, Michael. *How to Write a Book Proposal*. Writer's Digest Books, 1985. (Writer's Basic Bookshelf) (*A whole book on crafting nonfiction book proposals, with information applying to all questions and many ideas for books.*)

Lee, Marshall. *Bookmaking: The Illustrated Guide to Design, Production, Editing*. R. R. Bowker, 1979. (*Questions #7, 10: A classic. See Chapters 38 and 40 for brief, clear explanations of how editors acquire and edit; also Chapters 31, 39, and 41 for how editors work with design, production, and marketing.*)

Literary Market Place with Names and Numbers. R. R. Bowker, annual. (*Essential for publisher research on all questions.*)

Mayer, Debby. *Literary Agents: A Writer's Guide*. Poets & Writers, 1988. (*Question #11: See "Rights for Sale: 22 Different Markets for a Successful Trade Book."*)

McCormack, Thomas. *The Fiction Editor*. St. Martin's, 1988. (*How fiction editors work.*)

Mehitabel's Books and Supplies for Writers, Editors, and Publishers. P.O. Box 60357, Palo Alto, CA 94306. (*Good mail-order source for all books listed here.*)

Meredith, Scott. *Writing to Sell*. Harper & Row, 1987. (*Question #1: Advice from the literary agent on crafting all aspects to the novel, with an eye to what sells.*)

Meyer, Carol. *The Writer's Survival Manual: The Complete Guide to Getting Your Book Published Right*. Crown, 1982. (*Useful information on all questions.*)

Petersen, Clarence. *The Bantam Story: Thirty Years of Paperback Publishing*. Bantam, 1975. (*Question #10: Bantam editors at work.*)

Plotnik, Arthur. *The Elements of Editing: A Modern Guide for Editors and Journalists*. Macmillan, 1982. (*Question #7: A valuable how-to book for editors and writers on taking a manuscript apart.*)

Poets & Writers, Inc. *The Writing Business: A Poets & Writers Handbook.* 1985. (*Very useful for all questions, with chapters such as "How to Get Out of the Slush Pile," "What a Writer Should Know About Book Design," etc.*)

Publishers Weekly. R. R. Bowker, weekly magazine. Available at most libraries or write for subscription: Box 1979, Marion, OH 43305-1979. (*The single best source for up-to-date information on editors, books, and publishers.*)

Reed, Kit. *Revision.* Writer's Digest Books, 1989. (*Question #7: A guide to revising fiction.*)

Regnery, Henry. *Memoirs of a Dissident Publisher.* Regnery Gateway, 1979. (*Another editor at work.*)

Skillin, M., and R. Gay. *Words into Type.* Prentice-Hall, 1974. (*Question #1: Easy-to-digest copyediting classic, with a superb index.*)

Society of Children's Book Writers Bulletin. P.O. Box 296, Mar Vista Station, Los Angeles, CA 90066. (*Membership open to published and unpublished writers; each bulletin contains current information on editors. Or, investigate the publications from organizations more relevant to you, such as Mystery Writers of America [236 W. 27th St., New York, NY 10001] or Romance Writers of America [5206 FM 1960, W #208, Houston, TX 77069].*)

Strunk, William, Jr., and E.B. White. *The Elements of Style.* Macmillan, 1979. (*Question #1: This slim volume is still the best book on how to write clear prose.*)

Targ, William. *Indecent Pleasures.* Macmillan, 1975. (*Autobiography of editor who worked with Mario Puzo, Simone de Beauvoir, many others.*)

Whiteside, Thomas. *The Blockbuster Complex: Conglomerates, Show Business, and Book Publishing.* Wesleyan University Press, 1981. (*Questions #8, 11, 12.*)

Writer's Market and *Novel & Short Story Writer's Market.* Writer's

Digest Books, annual. (*Essential for publisher research on all questions.*)

Zinsser, William K. *On Writing Well: An Informal Guide to Writing Nonfiction.* Harper & Row, 1980. (*Question #1: Classic companion to Strunk and White.*)

INDEX

Other Books of Interest

Annual Market Books
    Artist's Market, edited by Susan Conner $18.95
    Children's Writer's & Illustrator's Market, edited by Connie Eidenier (paper) $14.95
    Novel & Short Story Writer's Market, edited by Laurie Henry (paper) $17.95
    Photographer's Market, edited by Connie Eidenier $19.95
    Poet's Market, by Judson Jerome $17.95
    Songwriter's Market, edited by Julie Whaley $17.95
    Writer's Market, edited by Glenda Neff $22.95
General Writing Books
    Beginning Writer's Answer Book, edited by Kirk Polking (paper) $12.95
    Beyond Style: Mastering the Finer Points of Writing, by Gary Provost $15.95
    How to Write a Book Proposal, by Michael Larsen $10.95
    Knowing Where to Look: The Ultimate Guide to Research, by Lois Horowitz (paper) $15.95
    Spider Spin Me a Web: Lawrence Block on Writing Fiction, by Lawrence Block $16.95
    12 Keys to Writing Books that Sell, by Kathleen Krull (paper) $12.95
    The 29 Most Common Writing Mistakes & How to Avoid Them, by Judy Delton $9.95
    Word Processing Secrets for Writers, by Michael A. Banks & Ansen Dibell (paper) $14.95
    The Writer's Digest Guide to Manuscript Formats, by Buchman & Groves $16.95
Nonfiction Writing
    How to Sell Every Magazine Article You Write, by Lisa Collier Cool (paper) $11.95
    The Writer's Digest Handbook of Magazine Article Writing, edited by Jean M. Fredette $15.95
    Writing Creative Nonfiction, by Theodore A. Rees Cheney $15.95
Fiction Writing
    The Art & Craft of Novel Writing, by Oakley Hall $16.95
    Characters & Viewpoint, by Orson Scott Card $12.95
    Dare to Be a Great Writer: 329 Keys to Powerful Fiction, by Leonard Bishop $15.95
    Dialogue, by Lewis Turco $12.95
    Fiction is Folks: How to Create Unforgettable Characters, by Robert Newton Peck (paper) $8.95
    Handbook of Short Story Writing: Vol 1, by Dickson and Smythe (paper) $9.95
    Handbook of Short Story Writing: Vol. II, edited by Jean M. Fredette $15.95
    One Great Way to Write Short Stories, by Ben Nyberg $14.95
    Plot, by Ansen Dibell $12.95
    Revision, by Kit Reed $13.95
    Writing the Modern Mystery, by Barbara Norville $15.95
    Writing the Novel: From Plot to Print, by Lawrence Block (paper) $9.95
Special Interest Writing Books
    Comedy Writing Secrets, by Melvin Helitzer $16.95
    The Complete Book of Scriptwriting, by J. Michael Straczynski (paper) $10.95
    Editing Your Newsletter, by Mark Beach (paper) $18.50
    Families Writing, by Peter Stillman (paper) $15.95
    How to Write Romances, by Phyllis Taylor Pianka $13.95

How to Write Tales of Horror, Fantasy & Science Fiction, edited by J.N. Williamson $15.95
How to Write & Sell Your Personal Experiences, by Lois Duncan (paper) $9.95
How to Write Western Novels, by Matt Braun $13.95
The Poet's Handbook, by Judson Jerome (paper) $9.95
Successful Scriptwriting, by Jurgen Wolff & Kerry Cox $18.95
Writing for Children & Teenagers, 3rd Edition, by Lee Wyndham & Arnold Madison (paper) $12.95
The Writing Business
A Beginner's Guide to Getting Published, edited by Kirk Polking $11.95
The Complete Guide to Self-Publishing, by Tom & Marilyn Ross (paper) $16.95
How to Sell & Re-Sell Your Writing, by Duane Newcomb $11.95
How to Write Irresistible Query Letters, by Lisa Collier Cool $11.95
How to Write with a Collaborator, by Hal Bennett with Michael Larsen, $11.95
How You Can Make $25,000 a Year Writing (No Matter Where You Live), by Nancy Edmonds Hanson $15.95
Time Management for Writers, by Ted Schwarz $10.95

To order directly from the publisher, include $2.50 postage and handling for 1 book and 50¢ for each additional book. Allow 30 days for delivery.
Writer's Digest Books, 1507 Dana Avenue, Cincinnati, Ohio 45207
Credit card orders call TOLL-FREE
1-800-543-4644 (Outside Ohio)
1-800-551-0884 (Ohio only)
Prices subject to change without notice.

Write to this same address for information on *Writer's Digest* magazine, Writer's Digest Book Club, Writer's Digest School, and Writer's Digest Criticism Service.